'So I shall tell you a story . . .'

Encounters with Beatrix Potter

'So I shall tell you a story . . .'

ENCOUNTERS WITH BEATRIX POTTER

Selected and introduced
by Judy Taylor

FREDERICK WARNE

For Libby

FREDERICK WARNE

Published by the Penguin Group
27 Wrights Lane, London W8 5TZ, England
Penguin Books USA Inc., 375 Hudson Street, New York, N.Y. 10014, USA
Penguin Books Australia Ltd, Ringwood, Victoria, Australia
Penguin Books Canada Ltd, 10 Alcorn Avenue, Toronto, Ontario, Canada M4V 3B2
Penguin Books (N.Z.) Ltd, 182–190 Wairau Road, Auckland 10, New Zealand

Penguin Books Ltd, Registered Offices: Harmondsworth, Middlesex, England

First published 1993
1 3 5 7 9 10 8 6 4 2

Notes and introductions copyright © Judy Taylor, 1993

Copyright information for individual pieces is given on pages 223–4
which constitute an extension of this copyright page

Beatrix Potter's original illustrations copyright ©
Frederick Warne & Co., 1902, 1903, 1904, 1905, 1906, 1907, 1908, 1909, 1910, 1911, 1912,
1913, 1917, 1918, 1921, 1929, 1930, 1955, 1972, 1987, 1989
New reproductions of Beatrix Potter's book illustrations copyright ©
Frederick Warne & Co., 1987
Copyright in all countries signatory to the Berne Convention

British Library Cataloguing in Publication Data available

ISBN 0 7232 4025 6

Printed and bound in Great Britain by William Clowes Limited,
Beccles and London

CONTENTS

INTRODUCTION

'Eastwood, Dunkeld. Sep 4th '93. My dear Noel, I don't know what to write to you, *so I shall tell you a story* about four little rabbits whose names were – Flopsy, Mopsy, Cotton-tail and Peter . . .'

Beatrix Potter's story, first written in a picture letter and then published in book form in 1901, became the best-selling children's book of all time and *The Tale of Peter Rabbit* still heads the lists a century later. Although it is fifty years since Beatrix died, there is ever-increasing interest in this intriguing woman and in her achievements. In this decade alone her life story has been told in straightforward biography, through selections of her letters and on film for television. Exhibitions of her watercolours, her sketches and her book illustrations attract large audiences wherever they are shown. Sales of her books multiply each year, as do the number of languages into which her stories are translated. Characters from her books feature in an ever-lengthening list of merchandise products sold across the world.

Seeking to isolate the reason for this continuing appeal I started to collect all I could find that has been written on Beatrix Potter and her books. The pieces were scattered through ancient newspapers and magazines (some long defunct), in diaries and memoirs, in anthologies of essays published in the USA, New Zealand, Canada and Australia, as well as in Japan, France and the United Kingdom. The amount of material is phenomenal. Some of it is crank rubbish, much of it is fascinating, interesting and amusing, but reading it confirms only that Beatrix Potter herself has captured the interest of an extraordinarily wide range of people and that each of them has their own interpretation of her stories.

Then came the offer of the publication of my own choice from the collection. It was a temptation I could not resist. The task of selection, however, proved far more difficult than I expected. An obvious first inclusion would surely be the 24 December 1903 review of *The Tailor of Gloucester* in *The Tailor and Cutter*, the paper the mouse on the cover of the book is reading. But it is mainly a long-winded summary of the plot, unusual only in that the tailor sits by the fire 'and doses' and Simpkin is described as the tailor's 'one earthly attendant'. It was more interesting to discover that the review was preceded by articles on 'Juvenile Coat Making' and 'Trouser Cuffs – a possibility'.

This early review had led me to look at others, but the reviewing of children's books in the early 1900s was not the sophisticated art it became for all too short a time in the 1960s. *The Times Literary Supplement* noticed children's books then; however, it was mainly in the 'yet another of Miss Potter's endearing books' mode (*Appley Dapply's Nursery Rhymes*, 1917). Another publication with regular notices for the Potter books as they were published was *The Bookman*, 'a monthly journal for book readers', but these were again short summaries of the plot rather than reviews. They usually ended with a comment about the publisher: 'These Chelsea-china-like books are Messrs. Warne & Co.'s annual marvels' (*The Tale of Two Bad Mice*, 1905) and 'Five and three-quarters by four and one-quarter inches, the publishers tell us these little books are. How much of the heart of the nursery can be caught within that amount of space!' (*The Tale of Mrs. Tiggy-Winkle*, 1905). I decided not to include reviews.

There were in the grand pile of articles and extracts a number of personal recollections of meetings with Beatrix Potter, too many to include them all and they became somewhat repetitive. There were enough child reactions to the Potter Books to make an entire volume on their own. And I was attracted to a number of the pieces by their titles alone – 'Miss Potter and the Little Rubbish', 'Happiness is a Warm Hedgehog', 'Sis Beatrix', 'Mr Tod: the Case for the Psychologist's Couch' – but the enjoyment of seeing the titles on the contents page was not a good enough reason for inclusion.

When the agony of the first-selection-to-a-given-length was over there remained some important aspects of Beatrix Potter's life and work that seemed only to have been mentioned in the context of longer works and not in shorter articles – her involvement in the early merchandise, her close association with the National Trust, the inspiration she has offered to other artists, the many unauthorized editions of her books. To present a more rounded picture of my subject I would need to commission new pieces. So Graham Greene's 1933 essay is joined by Brian Alderson's account of the merchandise, Marianne Moore's poem by Susan Denyer's history of Beatrix Potter and the National Trust, Maurice Sendak's defence of *Peter Rabbit* by Nicholas Garland's musing on Potter in political cartoons, and Alison Smithson's linking of Potter's use of space with the architects of the Modern Movement by Selwyn Goodacre's discussion of his collection of Potter 'piracies', and so on. The articles are presented in chronological order, either of the episode recounted or of first publication, and I have corrected the spelling throughout (it is surprising how many people have written about Mr Macgregor). As the Potter attraction continues to intrigue me, my hope is that these chosen encounters with Beatrix Potter and her little books will engage your interest, too.

JUDY TAYLOR

AUTHOR'S ACKNOWLEDGEMENTS

In addition to the many people who responded to my requests for help in tracking down Potter articles and to those authors whom I approached for permission to cut or to extract, I should in particular like to thank Pat Adam, Margaret Coughlan, Josefina de Vasconcellos (Josephine Banner), David Higginbottom, Libby Joy, Margaret Payne, Jeannine Laughlin-Porter (on Brian Alderson's behalf), Judith St. John, Tish Wilson and many members of the Beatrix Potter Society.

From an article by Maurice Sendak in Publishers' Weekly,
11 July 1966

When I recently read Beatrix Potter's books in chronological order, I became aware of a most curious phenomenon. Her voice in *Peter Rabbit* seems to be on normal 'ear level', but thereafter it becomes tiny, sharp as a needle, and, wonder of wonders, drops below ear level. Peter speaks from somewhere near your head, but the voices in *The Tailor of Gloucester* come from somewhere under the rug. By the time of *The Tale of Two Bad Mice*, the author has perfected her 'miniature' voice; it is a kind of ventriloquist act that scales the voice down to mouse size. This could be dismissed as an aberration peculiar to me. Be that as it may, when I read *The Pie and the Patty-Pan* – my favorite Potter – her voice is dog-and-cat-size.

In 1921 Anne Carroll Moore was sponsored by the American Committee for Devastated France to visit children's libraries in northern France and to arrange for new books to be sent to them. On her way home to New York she went for a two-week holiday to the Lake District.
The following account of Anne Carroll Moore's meetings with Beatrix Potter is taken from her contribution to The Art of Beatrix Potter *by Leslie Linder and W. A. Herring (Warne, 1955; now out of print). In 1952 she had received a letter inviting her to write the Introduction to this collection of previously unpublished drawings. 'I am honored to be asked to write an Appreciation (Beatrix Potter needs no Introduction),' she replied.*

MEETING BEATRIX POTTER

ANNE CARROLL MOORE, 1955

MY STORY BEGINS with the discovery of *The Tailor of Gloucester* among the new children's books sent over from London to an American children's library at Christmas-time 1903.

Far and few were the new books for little children at the turn of the century. Here was one of such exceptional quality and charm that it could be shared on equal terms with the head of the art department, with which this children's library was vitally connected, and the children to whom I first read it aloud in the children's room of the Pratt Institute Free Library in Brooklyn, New York. I have continued to read it every Christmas since then and it has lost none of its freshness as a work of art or as a Christmas story. . . .

I have always been glad that my own first impressions of Beatrix Potter as an artist were taken from *The Tailor of Gloucester* and from *Squirrel Nutkin*, published in the same year, rather than from *Peter Rabbit*. The individuality of character and setting of each little book remains clearer in mind in consequence and the value of her contribution to children's books, as

her own direct communication of the natural world to children, more fully appreciated. To me they have always been Beatrix Potter's books rather than the Peter Rabbit books.

First visual impressions haunt the memory. I met Peter Rabbit for the first time in a hideous pirated American edition bearing all the stigmata of the new comic strip that was filling the vacuum before American publishers began to give any attention to the production of children's books as works of art. Peter Rabbit lent himself so readily to imitation, caricature and exploitation as a comic character as to obscure his importance to an educational world in which nature and art had been dead for a very long time. The important thing about Peter Rabbit was that he was alive and true to the nature of a rabbit, as was quickly recognized by the children as soon as the authorized English edition with Beatrix Potter's own pictures took its place in their library. Children who had never read before burst into reading as they turned the pages just as they did in hundreds of American homes where Peter Rabbit was taken to bed every night.

From the intimacy of daily association with children and their books in Brooklyn I went to New York, at the height of a fresh tide of immigration, to offer a similar natural free access to books, without age limit, in the children's rooms of the New York Public Library and its many branches. These were largely in foreign neighborhoods but my confidence in picture books as first aids in creating a spontaneous desire to read was now firmly established.

Picture books were indispensable. . . .

The First World War brought a shortage of picture books which called for serious measures of conservation on the part of the library. Children must not be deprived of enjoyment of the books but the life of each book must be prolonged by loving care and a renewed sense of its value on the part of everybody. The response of children and librarians was a wonderful tribute to the books of Caldecott, Kate Greenaway, Leslie Brooke and Beatrix Potter.

At the end of the war no visitor was more welcome than Mr Fruing Warne, of Frederick Warne and Company, who came straight from the ship to the library and who brought good news of the reprinting of old favorites and the promise of new books from Beatrix Potter and Leslie Brooke. Then he told me that Beatrix Potter lived in the Lake District and that the illustrations for several of her books were from familiar scenes near her home, that the animals were all from living models – many of them her pets.

But when I asked where Beatrix Potter lived in the Lake District, Mr Warne said that her publishers could give no personal information about her. 'She is very averse to publicity of any kind,' he said. 'She is married now but continues to use her own name for her books. They have been remarkably successful. She has bought a farm from the royalties of *Peter Rabbit* and others.' Mr Warne had given me the first clue to the mystery of Beatrix Potter.

A year later I paid a return visit to Mr Warne in Bedford Court, where he proved as gracious a host in London as he had been a visitor in New York, taking me behind the scenes to see new books in the making and to the shipping department to discover *Peter Rabbit* and *Benjamin Bunny* in French.

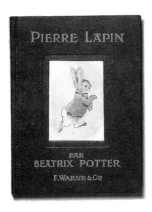

I had just come from searching the bookshops of Paris for picture books for the children's libraries which had been opened in wooden *baraques* on the ruins of homes and schools in northern France. Picture books, good picture books, seemed more important than ever before and translations of those with universal appeal an imperative need of the time. That Beatrix Potter's publishers were recognizing the importance of her work by translation was good news. Since *Pierre Lapin* and *Jeannot Lapin* were not yet available in France, I had the pleasure of ordering fifty copies to be sent to La Bibliothéque Populaire de Soissons, knowing well with what joy they would be received in the villages which were then being served by that library with the assistance of an American committee.

Before leaving Mr Warne's office I told him that I was to spend the next fortnight in Grasmere and that I wished to write to Beatrix Potter from there introducing myself. 'I can only wish you luck,' Mr Warne said but he gave me a slip of paper on which he had written Mrs William Heelis, Sawrey, Ambleside. From the Moss

Grove at Grasmere I wrote Mrs Heelis a letter telling her of American children and French children and their love of picture books. I told her of my delight in finding *Pierre Lapin* and *Jeannot Lapin* in London and I spoke of some beautiful photographs of French children and their grandmothers looking at picture books together. Would she like to see the pictures? By return came the following letter:

Dear Miss Moore   JUNE 24. 21

We shall be very glad to see you. Can you come to lunch on Monday? It is not long notice, but a pity to miss fine weather; and we have not much hay cut at present. I wonder how you will get here? [Two pages of explicit directions follow with an offer to send to the Ferry should I choose to come by boat.]

Excuse a scribble, I have just come out of the hay – It is uncommonly warm!

Yours sincerely,
Beatrix Heelis

I like the French translations, it is like reading some one else's work – refreshing.

On that beautiful June morning I chose to walk up the long hill leading from the Ferry to the village of Sawrey. Wild roses were blooming in the hedgerows and the air was fragrant with new-mown hay. And suddenly, just as I had hoped she might, Beatrix Heelis came 'out of the hay' to greet me, looking for all the world as Beatrix Potter should look. She was wearing a broad-brimmed straw hat and she carried a rake in her hand. On her feet were Lancashire clogs with buckles. Her sturdy figure was dressed for the hay field and not for company. Her bright blue eyes sparkled with merriment and her smile was that of a child who shares a secret, as indeed she did. She spoke with the tang of the north country. No

15

welcome could have been more cordial than hers to Hill Top Farm. Beatrix Heelis was in the mid-fifties at that time but her cheeks were rosy as those of a young girl and her eyes as clear and expectant.

Long before we came to the top of the lane leading to Castle Cottage I felt as if I had known her always. The familiar flower garden of her picture books tempted us to linger there, for the foxgloves were in their glory. 'But it's time for lunch,' said my hostess. 'Mr Heelis likes to be on time.' William Heelis, tall and gentle in manner, with the ease of a man who belonged to that countryside, had just come from his law office in Ambleside.

I have no recollection of anything we ate or talked about at that midday meal but I was conscious of a fine reserve of quiet humor on the part of Mr Heelis. He showed no surprise, but looked amused, when his wife turned to me with an expectant look and said, 'If Mr Heelis would drive you to Bowness afterward, couldn't you stay on for tea? It would give more time to look about.' I needed no urging to 'stay on'.

Looking about began with feeding Emily and Tapioca, leaders of a large family of turkeys, descendants of Charles the rooster, Pigling Bland and others. It meant seeing

Hill Top Farm as Jemima Puddle-Duck and Tom Kitten saw it.

Fascinating as it was to follow the farmyard trails with Beatrix Potter herself, the best was yet to come when from her study in Castle Cottage she brought out one portfolio after another and left me free to browse at will among the pencil sketches, pen-and-ink drawings, the crayons, the watercolors from which the pictures in her books had grown. 'I can see that you are enjoying yourself,' she said. 'My portfolios are not in order but I can always find what I'm looking for when I need it. You may choose any one you think your children in New York would like.'

When I chose a small watercolor of rabbits playing in the snow with their sleds, Beatrix Potter was reminded of sitting out in the scorching summer sunshine painting snow scenes for *The Tailor of Gloucester*. I was absorbed in a portfolio of wild flowers – bluebells, primroses, daisies – when my hostess left me for an hour. When she came back she brought a portfolio of the fungi drawings. 'I know these are good,' she said quietly. 'I made a great many of them, hoping they might illustrate a book I was not qualified to write. It needed a scientist. Some of the funguses are very rare. They made a fascinating study for a number of years. My eyes no longer permit me to do such fine work. I did enjoy finding them and painting them and they give me pleasure whenever I take time to look at them and recall the places they came from. The drawings fill seven portfolios and were done years before any of my books for children.'

Admiration for the exquisite watercolors, revealing the eye of the naturalist for each individual species and the feeling of the artist for the beauty and faery-like quality of the subject, led me to ask if she had ever exhibited her work. 'No,' Beatrix Potter replied. 'I have never cared to exhibit my work. Very few people have ever seen the funguses. I am happy to know that you appreciate them.' There was barely time to visit the dairy and watch Beatrix Heelis skim rich yellow cream for the strawberries which lent color and fragrance to our tea. Nowhere out of the Lake District would one find such a tea.

Behind the teapot, with Mr Heelis across the table, Beatrix Heelis turned to me, eyes sparkling with fun, and whispered, 'If you had a nightie and toothbrush, couldn't you stay all night?' Still dazed by all I'd seen that afternoon, I suddenly realized that the visit had turned into an adventure for Beatrix Potter herself as well as for me. I looked in vain for some sign of dissent or disapproval from Mr Heelis who must have heard the whisper. 'I think the nicest way of having company is to ask them to stay on after they come instead of before,' Mrs Heelis continued. 'You haven't seen the half of Hill Top and I want to look at the French pictures again and hear more about the New York children. Please stay with us.'

Who could resist such an invitation? As we rose from the tea-table it was Beatrix Potter who handed me a huge door key. The key to her own Hill Top Farm House. 'Now, run on down the lane and unlock the door and *rummage* to your heart's content and you'll be able to tell the children in New York that you've seen every nook and corner of Tom Kitten's House. You'll not be disturbed by any of Samuel Whiskers' relations. Enjoy yourself!'

And so I entered Hill Top Farm House alone and found it exactly as it is pictured in *The Roly-Poly Pudding* [later renamed *The Tale of Samuel Whiskers*] – the kitchen chimney up which Tom Kitten jumped, the cupboard where Moppet and Mittens were shut, the staircase on which Mrs Tabitha Twitchit pattered up and down, the very same carpet and curtains, the mysterious attic where Ribby and Tabitha heard the roly-poly noise. I opened doors, peeked into cupboards and chests until I began to hear roly-poly noises myself. Then it was I discovered one

after another the things Beatrix Potter had put into other books, the clock on the staircase, a chair in *The Tailor of Gloucester*, the very teacups the mice had peeped out from under, a wonderful old dresser. I explored the house all over again for signs of her own daily life there before she became Beatrix Heelis, and the house responded, as old houses will sometimes when one is quite alone and receptive.

As I locked the door and stepped into the lane, it was not of 'Samuel Whiskers and his wife on the run with a wheel-barrow' I was thinking but of Beatrix Potter herself. She seemed as completely identified with the old house as with the pictures I had seen in the portfolios. In giving me freedom to explore both myself, she had given me friendship and trust.

We took a long walk with Mr Heelis after that and watched the sun go down behind the Langdales from the top of the hill. Then back to Castle Cottage for a hot supper cooked by Beatrix Heelis herself.

The photographs of French children and their grandmothers enjoying pictures together led to many questions. Beatrix Potter had never been in France. 'I've never been out of the British Isles,' she said. When I told her of the old women I had seen who had chosen to live on in the ruins of their homes on their own land rather than take shelter with relatives or friends in the city, she exclaimed, 'That is just what I should do if my home was destroyed – stay on the land.' . . .

We visited the 'Ginger and Pickles' shop together next morning and before I went on my way we stopped at Hill Top Farm House where Beatrix Heelis inscribed a copy of *The Roly-Poly Pudding* with my name 'from "Beatrix Potter" in remembrance of Hill Top Farm, Sawrey, June 27, 1921'. It is the edition of larger size in which the book was first published.

'You will always be welcome at Hill Top whenever you come to England,' she said, 'and you may send any of the storytellers in your children's libraries. I know they would be coming for the sake of the children and not out of mere curiosity.'

It was in May 1937, after the Coronation celebrations in London, that I came to Hill Top again for a visit as memorable as, but entirely different from, the first round-the-clock one of 1921.

'It will be a pleasure and an interesting event to see you again,' Beatrix Heelis had written on May 4th. 'I wish you had been here this week – the country has been looking so lovely – cherry blossom, whitethorn, damson all out in bloom together . . . The bluebells . . . will be out next week . . . The hawthorns will be very fine; buds just showing. I will show you the Troutbeck woods if we have time . . . I can send to meet the 5.15 at Windermere an old-fashioned black and green Talbot saloon and an aged chauffeur. We hope for a very fine pleasant visit this time.'

Whoever knows England at Coronation time will recall the afterglow of the great day in the villages. It still lingered in Sawrey. Beatrix Heelis, radiant at seventy, welcomed me in holiday mood. This time she came out of her Pringle Wood to tell me the bluebells were in bloom. The hedgerows were white with hawthorn, lilacs scented the air, and every garden in the village was bright with tulips and late daffodils.

There was much to talk about during the long first evening. Our sixteen-year-old friendship had been kept warm by exchange of letters and books at Christmas-time and at other times. Beatrix Heelis had bought one farm after another beyond the boundaries of Hill Top during those years. She had become a widely respected and honored sheep farmer of the north country. Had her interest in Herdwick sheep completely absorbed Beatrix Potter the creative

artist? If her letters had left a doubt it would have been dispelled by the talk of this evening and of days that followed.

'I want to show you the farms which have the most beautiful views,' she said. 'We'll take a drive every morning, rain or shine.' And so to Skelwith, Coniston, Little Langdale we were driven by the aged chauffeur who sat patiently waiting while we looked about old farms and cottages which seemed a part of the landscape.

The high point for me on that wonderful guided tour of the Lake District was reached at Troutbeck Park Farm where a sheep shearing was going on outside and a knot of shepherds had gathered from neighboring farms. Mrs Heelis regarded her sheep with an appraising eye to their condition after a hard winter. Few words were spoken but she exchanged greetings with each one of the shepherds and mingled with them to watch the shearing.

Inside the shepherd's cottage, high above the old-fashioned open cooking stove, hung a very large oil painting of sheep in the Scottish Highlands. 'It is one of my brother's paintings,' said Beatrix Heelis. 'It was too large for the room I set apart at Hill Top for his pictures. The shepherd's wife seems to enjoy having it here. She says it gives her a lift to look as far as Scotland when she feels she has too much to do.'

When I spoke of a fine old chest in another room of the cottage, Beatrix Heelis gave it a loving pat. 'I cannot resist the old oak cupboards and chests at an auction so I buy them and fit them in wherever I can.'

Troutbeck Park Farm stands at the head of the long curving Troutbeck Valley. Beyond it tower High Street and Ill Bell. I had often passed the lonely farm on my walks on the fells in the summer of 1906, the very summer Beatrix Potter was getting Hill Top Farm House ready to live in. . . .

That evening our talk was all of Troutbeck. It was then that Beatrix Heelis told me of her wanderings over Troutbeck fell, of the dance of the wild fell ponies about the thorn tree. 'It was finding their little fairy footmarks on the old drove road that first made me aware of the Fairy Caravan,' she said. She had wandered farther into the wilderness behind Troutbeck Tongue than I had, but for each of us as we had walked alone, without loneliness, there remained a memory of complete enchantment. . . .

Beatrix Potter rested in the afternoons and on one of them I explored Pringle Wood for signs of Pony Billy on 'the fairy hill of oaks'. 'How blue the bluebells were: a sea of soft pale blue; tree behind tree; and beneath the trees, wave upon wave, a blue sea of bluebells.'

On another day I wandered through Codlin Croft orchard with *The Fairy Caravan* and came back to read with fresh delight the conversation between Charles the cock and the hens, Selina Picka-corn, Tappie-tourie and Chucky-doddie. Rereading *The Fairy Caravan* at Hill Top led me to speak of its richness and variety, of its true relation to each one of the little books. 'It puts the very life of the England they came out of behind them and it gives Beatrix Potter her own place in it,' I said. 'You did not mention it when I was here before.'

'No, at that time I thought of it as too personal to be of interest to anyone else,' Beatrix Heelis replied. 'I am very slow about making up my mind about things. It takes years sometimes for an idea to take shape. It was so with several of the books – years between a picture letter idea and the book.'. . .

In A Sort of Life *(1971) Graham Greene recalled the books on his nursery shelves which interested him most. 'I have never lost my admiration for her [Beatrix Potter's] books and I have often reread her,' he wrote. He was twenty-eight when his essay on Beatrix Potter was first published, in the January 1933 edition of the monthly periodical,* The London Mercury.

BEATRIX POTTER: A CRITICAL ESTIMATE

GRAHAM GREENE, 1933

'IT IS SAID THAT the effect of eating too much lettuce is "soporific".' It is with some such precise informative sentence that one might have expected the great Potter saga to open, for the obvious characteristic of Beatrix Potter's style is a selective realism, which takes emotion for granted and puts aside love and death with a gentle detachment reminiscent of Mr E.M. Forster's. Her stories contain plenty of dramatic action, but it is described from the outside by an acute and unromantic observer, who never sacrifices truth for an effective gesture. As an example of Miss Potter's empiricism, her rigid adherence to what can be seen and heard, consider the climax of her masterpiece *The Roly-Poly Pudding* [later renamed *The Tale of Samuel Whiskers*], Tom Kitten's capture by the rats in the attic:

"Anna Maria," said the old man rat (whose name was Samuel Whiskers), – "Anna Maria, make me a kitten dumpling roly-poly pudding for my dinner."

"It requires dough and a pat of butter, and a rolling-pin," said Anna Maria, considering Tom Kitten with her head on one side.

"No," said Samuel Whiskers, "make it properly, Anna Maria, with breadcrumbs."

But in 1908, when *The Roly-Poly Pudding* was published, Miss

Potter was at the height of her power. She was not a born realist, and her first story [in fact it was her second] was not only romantic, it was historical. *The Tailor of Gloucester* opens:

> In the time of swords and periwigs and full-skirted coats with flowered lappets – when gentlemen wore ruffles, and gold-laced waistcoats of paduasoy and taffeta – there lived a tailor in Gloucester.

In the sharp details of this sentence, in the flowered lappets, there is a hint of the future Potter, but her first book is not only hampered by its period setting but by the presence of a human character. Miss Potter is seldom at her best with human beings (the only flaw in *The Roly-Poly Pudding* is the introduction in the final pages of the authoress in person), though with one human character she succeeded triumphantly. I refer, of course, to Mr McGregor, who made an elusive appearance in 1904 in *The Tale of Benjamin Bunny*, ran his crabbed earthmould way through *Peter Rabbit*, and met his final ignominious defeat in *The Flopsy Bunnies* in 1909. But the tailor of Gloucester cannot be compared with Mr McGregor. He is too ineffective and too virtuous, and the atmosphere of the story – snow and Christmas bells and poverty – is too Dickensian. Incidentally in Simpkin Miss Potter drew her only unsympathetic portrait of a cat. The ancestors of Tom Thumb and Hunca Munca play a humanitarian part. Their kind hearts are a little oppressive.

In the same year Miss Potter published *Squirrel Nutkin*. It is an unsatisfactory book, less interesting than her first, which was a good example of a bad *genre*. But in 1904, with the publication of *Two Bad Mice*, Miss Potter opened the series of her great comedies. In this story of Tom Thumb and Hunca Munca and their wanton havoc of a doll's house, the unmistakable Potter style first appears.

It is an elusive style, difficult to analyse. It owes something to alliteration:

Hunca Munca stood up in her chair, and chopped at the ham with another lead knife.

"It's as hard as the hams at the cheesemonger's," said Hunca Munca.

Something too it owes to the short paragraphs, which are fashioned with a delicate irony, not to complete a movement, but mutely to criticize the action by arresting it. The imperceptive pause allows the mind to take in the picture: the mice are stilled in their enraged attitudes for a moment, before the action sweeps forward.

Then there was no end to the rage and disappointment of Tom Thumb and Hunca Munca. They broke up the pudding, the lobsters, the pears and the oranges.

As the fish would not come off the plate, they put it into the red-hot crinkly paper fire in the kitchen; but it would not burn either.

It is curious that Beatrix Potter's method of paragraphing has never been imitated.

The last quotation shows another element of her later style, her love of a precise catalogue, her creation of atmosphere with still life. One remembers Mr McGregor's rubbish heap:

There were jam pots and paper bags, and mountains of chopped grass from the mowing machine (which always tasted oily), and some rotten vegetable marrows and an old boot or two.

The only indication in *Two Bad Mice* of a prentice hand is the sparsity of dialogue; her characters had not yet begun to utter those brief pregnant sentences, which have slipped, like proverbs, into common speech. Nothing in the early book equals Mr Jackson's, 'No teeth, no teeth, no teeth!'

In 1904 too *The Tale of Peter Rabbit*, the second of the great comedies, was published [in fact *Peter Rabbit* was published in 1902], closely followed by its sequel, *Benjamin Bunny*. In Peter and his cousin Benjamin Miss Potter created two epic personalities. The great characters of fiction are often paired: Quixote and Sancho, Pantagruel and Panurge, Pickwick and Weller, Benjamin and Peter. Peter was a neurotic, Benjamin worldly and imperturbable. Peter was warned by his mother, 'Don't go into Mr McGregor's garden: your Father had an accident there; he was put in a pie by Mrs McGregor.' But Peter went from stupidity rather than for adventure. He escaped from Mr McGregor by leaving his clothes behind, and the sequel, the story of how his clothes were recovered, introduces Benjamin, whose coolness and practicality are a foil to the nerves and clumsiness of his cousin. It was Benjamin who knew the way to enter a garden: 'It spoils people's clothes to squeeze under a gate; the proper way to get in, is to climb down a pear tree.' It was Peter who fell down head first.

From 1904 to 1908 were the vintage years in

comedy; to these years belong *The Pie and The Patty-Pan, The Tale of Tom Kitten, The Tale of Mrs. Tiggy-Winkle,* and only one failure, *Mr. Jeremy Fisher.* Miss Potter had found her right vein and her right scene. The novels were now set in Cumberland; the farms, the village shops, the stone walls, the green slope of Catbells became the background of her pictures and her prose. She was peopling a countryside. Her dialogue had become memorable because aphoristic:

> "I disapprove of tin articles in puddings and pies. It is most undesirable – (especially when people swallow in lumps!)"

She could draw a portrait in a sentence:

> . . . "my name is Mrs Tiggy-winkle; oh, yes if you please'm, I'm an excellent clear-starcher!"

And with what beautiful economy she sketched the first smiling villain of her gallery. Tom Kitten had dropped his clothes off the garden wall as the Puddle-Duck family passed:

> "Come! Mr Drake Puddle-Duck," said Moppet – "Come and help us to dress him! Come and button up Tom!"
> Mr Drake Puddle-Duck advanced in a slow sideways manner, and picked up the various articles.
> But he put them on *himself*! They fitted him even worse than Tom Kitten.
> "It's a very fine morning!" said Mr Drake Puddle-Duck.

Looking backward over the thirty years of Miss Potter's literary career, we see that the creation of Mr Puddle-Duck marked the beginning of a new period. At some time between 1907 and 1909 Miss Potter must have passed through an emotional ordeal which changed the character of her genius. It would be impertinent to inquire into the nature of the ordeal. Her case is curiously similar to that of Henry James. Something happened which shook their faith in appearance. From *The Portrait of a Lady* onwards, innocence deceived, the treachery of friends, became the theme of James's greatest stories. Madame Merle, Kate Croy, Madame de Vionnet, Charlotte Stant, these tortuous treacherous women are parallelled through the dark period of Miss Potter's art. 'A man can smile and smile and be a villain,' that, a little altered, was her recurrent message, expressed by her gallery of scoundrels: Mr Drake Puddle-Duck, the first and slightest, Mr Jackson, the least harmful with his passion for honey and his reiterated, 'No teeth, no teeth, no teeth!',

Samuel Whiskers, gross and brutal, and the 'gentleman with sandy whiskers' who may be identified with Mr Tod. With the publication of *Mr. Tod* in 1912, Miss Potter's pessimism reached its climax. But for the nature of her audience *Mr. Tod* would certainly have ended tragically. In *Jemima Puddle-Duck* the gentleman with sandy whiskers had at least a debonair impudence when he addressed his victim:

"... Before you commence your tedious sitting, I intend to give you a treat. Let us have a dinner-party all to ourselves!

"May I ask you to bring up some herbs from the farm-garden to make a savoury omelette? Sage and thyme, and mint and two onions, and some parsley. I will provide lard for the stuff – lard for the omelette," said the hospitable gentleman with sandy whiskers.

But no charm softens the brutality of Mr Tod and his enemy, the repulsive Tommy Brock. In her comedies Miss Potter had gracefully eliminated the emotions of love and death; it is the measure of her genius that when, in *The Tale of Mr. Tod*, they broke the barrier, the form of her book, her ironic style, remained unshattered. When she could not keep death out she stretched her technique to include it. Benjamin and Peter had grown up and married, and Benjamin's babies were stolen by Brock; the immortal pair, one still neurotic, the other knowing and imperturbable, set off to the rescue, but the rescue, conducted in darkness, from a house, 'something between a cave, a prison, and a tumbledown pig-stye', compares grimly with an earlier rescue from Mr McGregor's sunny vegetable garden:

> The sun had set; an owl began to hoot in the wood. There were many unpleasant things lying about, that had much better have been buried; rabbit bones and skulls, and chickens' legs and other horrors. It was a shocking place, and very dark.

But *Mr. Tod*, for all the horror of its atmosphere, is indispensable. There are few fights in literature which can compare in excitement with the duel between Mr Tod and Tommy Brock (it was echoed by H. G. Wells in *Mr Polly*):

> Everything was upset except the kitchen table.
> And everything was broken, except the mantelpiece and the kitchen fender. The crockery was smashed to atoms.
> The chairs were broken, and the window, and the clock fell with a crash, and there were handfuls of Mr Tod's sandy whiskers.

The vases fell off the mantelpiece, the canisters fell off the shelf;
the kettle fell off the hob. Tommy Brock put his foot in a jar of
raspberry jam.

Mr. Tod marked the distance which Miss Potter had travelled since
the ingenuous romanticism of *The Tailor of Gloucester*. The next
year with *The Tale of Pigling Bland*, the period of the great
near-tragedies came to an end. There was something of the same
squalor, and the villain, Mr Peter Thomas Piperson, was not less
terrible than Mr Tod, but the book ended on a lyrical note, as
Pigling Bland escaped with Pig-wig:

> They ran, and they ran, and they ran down the hill, and across
> a short cut on level green turf at the bottom, between pebble beds
> and rushes.
> They came to the river, they came to the bridge – they crossed
> it hand in hand –

It was the nearest Miss Potter had approached to a conventional
love story. The last sentence seemed a promise that the cloud had
lifted, that there was to be a return to the style of the earlier
comedies. But *Pigling Bland* was published in 1913. Through the
years of war the author was silent, and for many years after it was
over, only a few books of rhyme appeared. These showed that Miss
Potter had lost none of her skill as an artist, but left the great
question of whither her genius was tending unanswered. Then,
after seventeen years, at the end of 1930, *Little Pig Robinson* was
published.

The scene was no longer Cumberland but Devonshire and the
sea. The story, more than twice as long as *Mr. Tod*, was diffuse and
undramatic. The smooth smiling villain had disappeared and taken
with him the pungent dialogue, the sharp detail, the light of
common day. Miss Potter had not returned to the great comedies.
She had gone on beyond the great near-tragedies to her *Tempest*. No
tortured Lear nor strutting Antony could live on Prospero's island,

among the sounds and sweet airs and cloud-capt towers. Miss Potter too had reached her island, the escape from tragedy, the final surrender of imagination to safe serene fancy:

. . . a stream of boiling water flowed down the silvery strand.

The shore was covered with oysters. Acid drops and sweets grew upon the trees. Yams, which are a sort of sweet potato, abounded ready cooked. The bread-fruit tree grew iced cakes and muffins, ready baked . . .

It was all very satisfying for a Pig Robinson, but in that rarefied air no bawdy Tommy Brock could creep to burrow, no Benjamin pursue his feud between the vegetable-frames, no Puddle-Duck could search in wide-eyed innocence for a 'convenient dry nesting-place'.

When this piece was included in Graham Greene's Collected Essays *(Bodley Head, 1969) he added the following note: 'On the publication of this essay I received a somewhat acid letter from Miss Potter correcting certain details.* Little Pig Robinson, *although the last published of her books, was in fact the first written. She denied that there had been any emotional disturbance at the time she was writing* Mr. Tod: *she was suffering however from the after-effects of flu. In conclusion she deprecated sharply "the Freudian school" of criticism.'*

'The World of Beatrix Potter' was published on 21 January 1943 in The Listener, *a BBC weekly magazine which ran from January 1929 until the end of 1990.*

THE WORLD OF BEATRIX POTTER

JANET ADAM SMITH, 1943

FOR MANY FAMILIES, the shortage of Beatrix Potters this Christmas was a hardship far worse than the disappearance of crackers, jellies and rubber toys. But it is for more than selfish reasons that we can look forward to the days when they will be again as plentiful in bookshops as nuts on Owl Island. For they give, not only immediate delight, but contact – for many readers, almost their only

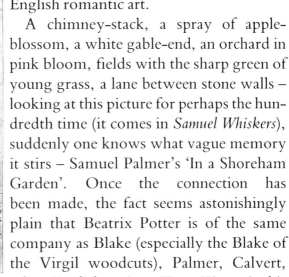

contact – with the purest tradition of English romantic art.

A chimney-stack, a spray of apple-blossom, a white gable-end, an orchard in pink bloom, fields with the sharp green of young grass, a lane between stone walls – looking at this picture for perhaps the hundredth time (it comes in *Samuel Whiskers*), suddenly one knows what vague memory it stirs – Samuel Palmer's 'In a Shoreham Garden'. Once the connection has been made, the fact seems astonishingly plain that Beatrix Potter is of the same company as Blake (especially the Blake of the Virgil woodcuts), Palmer, Calvert, Bewick, and a host of earlier English artists. Tom Kitten in his finery bursting 'up the rockery by degrees' belongs to the same world as the mermaid that Thomas Toft the seventeenth-century potter put on his plates; the sage that Jemima Puddle-Duck nibbled

33

to make her own stuffing, the crab-apples and green fir-cones with which Nutkin played ninepins, take us back to the strawberries and columbines of Elizabethan embroideries. Beatrix Potter has in full measure Samuel Palmer's gift of suffusing a landscape with innocence, happiness and serenity – not by smearing a vague 'atmosphere' over everything, but by particularizing. You can count every stone of her garden walls as you can count every stook and sheaf in Palmer's drawings of harvest-fields. Jeremy Fisher may wear galoshes, but he and the stickleback and the water-beetle are drawn with the affectionate precision that we find in Bewick's woodcuts, and rarely meet in other children's animal storybooks. Inanimate objects too, porridge-bowls, garden-rakes and kitchen-ranges, are shown with a similar love and accuracy, and in this Beatrix Potter recalls an artist of our own day, Frances Hodgkins, in whose pictures a bowl, a plough, or a water-jug dominates a whole scene.

Beatrix Potter's rakes and baskets are not just adjuncts to her stories, nor are her landscapes simply backgrounds. Objects and landscapes both speak of a particular world – not just a particular place, though they certainly do that, but a place where a particular life is lived. With talk of Newlands, Little Town and Catbells (in *Mrs. Tiggy-Winkle*), Miss Potter has told us *where* her world is; Jemima Puddle-Duck's farmhouse is surely in Borrowdale, and Owl Island on Derwentwater. The carved chair of Old Mr Brown, the flowery cups under which the Tailor of Gloucester discovered Simpkin's mice, the wide-woven garden basket on which the cat sat imprisoning Benjamin and Peter, the stone wall of Mr McGregor's garden, and the clogs in which Benjamin made footmarks all over Mr McGregor's newly-sown lettuce-bed – these can still be seen in Cumberland farms, and you can buy baskets or clogs (though not as small as Benjamin's) on market-day in Appleby or Penrith. They are some of the images of the independent, hospitable, hardy and largely self-sufficient life that people still lead in the dales, where every action has its due season and order, where the handling of a lamb or a scythe, the building of a stone wall or a sheep-fold, are not just jobs to be done, but mysteries to be respected. This life is implicit in nearly all Beatrix Potter's books; perhaps, indeed, it is the main reason why the books are remembered and loved long after we have forgotten the details of the entrancing adventures. Books like the Moldy Warp [*Grey Rabbit*] series have only the story to carry them: no one would remember fondly their suburban world of arty-modern furniture and mock antiques.

Here, too, Beatrix Potter joins hands with Samuel Palmer. Her pictures are actual Cumberland and Westmorland, as Palmer's are actual Kent; but the Kentish cornfields and the Cumberland stone walls speak also of love, innocence and mystery. Her country, at once so solidly and practically actual, yet suffused in magic light, has nothing to do with the structure of manor, squire and gentry that we get so charmingly in Caldecott's illustrations to nursery books: in it we are conscious only of the older, earthier, mightier rhythms of seasons, crops, animals and weather. And in this again Beatrix Potter is a true artist for the English; who, however towny, have nearly all at heart an instinct that the best life exists somewhere in the country, even if they have no wish to look for it. She is never nostalgic about this life, for it does still survive, not only in the dales and fells, but also in the eyes of every child who looks at fir-cones, columbines, and cart-wheels with absorption and delight: 'He from these lands of terrifying mottoes / Makes world as innocent as Beatrix Potter's' – perhaps Auden was saying all this with a poet's conciseness. Innocent indeed is her world, not only with a child's innocence, but with the innocence of an old and necessary wisdom.

*When Janet Adam Smith sent her article to Beatrix Potter she received
the following reply:*

To Janet Adam Smith   Feb 2.43

Dear Madam,

I am obliged for the 'Listener' – some one had already sent me a
copy which I read with mingled gratitude and stupefaction – the
writer seems to know a deal more about the inception of the Peter
Rabbit books than I do! When first published another outraged
authoress (and her publisher) said they were a crib of a horrid little
book called "Little Black Sambo". Now you say they are founded
on the work of the Immortals – all names which I revere, but the
only one of them I really tried to copy was Randolph Caldecott, and
you say there is no resemblance.

I am very glad the
books have given so
much pleasure and
continue to be useful. I
can no longer see to
overwork my eyes;
and I think I have
"done my bit"; –
unconsciously – trying
to copy nature – with-
out affectation or
swelled head.

Its well I do not depend on the BBC – they "conveyed" one of
my books without asking, and paid – was it £2.2.0 or £1.10.0? I
wonder what they paid you.

Again thanking you I remain

Yrs sincerely
H. B. Heelis (Mrs W. Heelis)

PS When a person has been nearly thirty years married it's not
ingratiating to get an envelope addressed to 'Miss'.

DRAFT OF A LETTER TO MRS HEELIS   FEB 3 43

Dear Madam,

I am writing at once to say how very sorry I am for addressing you wrongly the other day when I sent you a copy of *The Listener* with my article. I thought perhaps that in matters concerned with your books you might prefer 'Miss Potter' – I do apologize sincerely for my mistake.

I am so sorry too that some sentences in my article seem to have caused misunderstanding. Of course I did not mean to say that your delightful books are 'founded' on anybody else's work at all – it would indeed be impertinence in a stranger to talk about this, or to say that any other artist influenced you – that was not at all what I meant when I spoke of you 'being of the same company' as Samuel Palmer, Calvert etc. etc. What I meant was that your illustrations often give the reader the same kind of pleasure as their pictures do, and that your way of looking at Nature was the way the truest English artists have looked at Nature. I read somewhere the other day that Constable, asked by a friend what he was trying to do to a picture he was working on, said 'I am trying to put the Dewy Freshness into it' – that phrase, the Dewy Freshness, did also seem to describe some of your illustrations.

Please forgive this explanation, but I did not want you to think that I was talking about the origins of your work – which would indeed be an impertinent thing for me to do. And please forgive my unintentioned discourtesy in addressing you wrongly, and accept once more our warmest thanks for all the pleasure you have given, & shall give us.

Yours, etc.
[Mrs Roberts (Janet Adam Smith)]

TO MRS ROBERTS   FEB. 8.43

Dear Mrs Roberts,

"There is nothing new under the sun". We seem so much 'at cross purposes' that its not much use pursuing the subject. I have too *much* common sense to resent a suggestion that my painting-manner is not original & founded upon another painter's manner, but I think it is silly to suggest it is founded on Constable – a great artist with a broad style. When I was young it was still permissable [sic] to admire the PreRaphaelites; their somewhat niggling but absolutely genuine admiration for copying natural details did certainly influence me; also F. Walker & his school and Hunt.

You write nicely, but in this case you have been trying to write an article without quite enough knowledge. Try and write some articles about country wayside objects – if you are a beginner – and write them for your own children – that is the secret of good writing – have something to say – and write with an end in view. I must not say write "with a purpose" because that is next door to a moral – and Miss Edgeworth (who did influence me!) is out of fashion.

And for goodness sake don't write any more rubbish about me.

I remain yrs sincerely

Beatrix Heelis

In 1991, when requesting Janet Adam Smith's permission to include
The Listener *article and her draft letter in this collection, I asked her*
how she felt about it all now, nearly fifty years later.

When I wrote the article in 1943, I was living with my children in Penrith, on the edge of the Lake District, where we had gone on the outbreak of war in 1939. Now a resident in the Lakes, and no mere holiday-maker, I realized as I read the books to my children how truly Beatrix Potter's pictures had caught the enduring character of this

countryside. The white farmhouses, the stone walls sprouting ferns and flowers, the slates on the fellside that marked the entrance to old mine workings (or Mrs Tiggy-Winkle's snug home) were there in our lives as well as in the books. I knew little of Beatrix Potter except that she lived somewhere beyond Windermere and had been a friend of my parents' great friend, Canon Rawnsley. I knew nothing of her horror of publicity, or how upset she had been a year or two earlier by Graham Greene's admiring and affectionate joke, when he wrote of her *oeuvre* in the way old-fashioned critics once wrote of Shakespeare: the great comedies (*Two Bad Mice*, *Tom Kitten*); the 'dark' comedies, with their Jamesian hint of treachery (*Jemima Puddle-Duck*); the near-tragedy of *Mr. Tod*. Mrs Heelis thought she was being mocked.

My article was written with enthusiasm and love. I hoped it would please Beatrix Potter and sent her a copy. Then arrived the first of two letters from Mrs Heelis. I was appalled. How could she have so misunderstood me. I wrote back trying to explain that I had never meant her work was 'founded' on anybody else's; only that in the atmosphere conveyed by her pictures she was 'of the company' of Blake, Calvert and Samuel Palmer. Rashly, as I now see, I said her pictures had that quality of 'dewy freshness' a critic had found in Constable. Now she thought I was comparing her to Constable!

It was hopeless to explain further. She died a year after my article appeared. I was sad that words written in admiration should have caused such offence.

It was only forty years later, after reading *Beatrix Potter's Letters*, that I realized just why she had been so fierce with me. There she was at Sawrey, Mrs Heelis the farmer, expert on Herdwick sheep, vigilant benefactor of the National Trust – and here was an impertinent young woman breaking into her privacy, calling her Miss Potter, praising the little books which now bored her, and apparently making claims for her pictures that she found ridiculous. I still cringe when I read her letters, and I am still sad at the misunderstanding.

*Researching for Beatrix Potter: Artist, Storyteller and
Countrywoman in 1985 I came across the surprising
report that Beatrix Potter and her husband, William Heelis,
had contemplated migrating to Canada after the First
World War. At the time I was unable to trace the source
of this story but here it is now – from the Toronto* Globe & Mail
*of 4 February 1956, where it appeared under the headline
'How Peter Rabbit's Creator Nearly Became a Canadian'.*

WITH KIND REGARDS

❧

E. M. CLELAND, 1956

DURING THE LAST war I was spending a leave with some new friends
in the Lake District and, never having been there before, they took
me for a drive to show me the high spots, as it were. As we were
going through the village of Sawrey my hostess pointed out a stone
farmhouse and remarked: 'A woman lives there who's rather
famous in her way. Her name is Mrs Heelis. But years ago when
she was a Miss Beatrix Potter she wrote *Peter Rabbit* and a whole
series of wonderful books for children.'

I had not laid eyes on a Peter Rabbit book since my own
worn-out copy vanished about the time I started school, but
instantly I remembered a host of old friends with names like Peter
Rabbit and Timmy Tiptoes and Jeremy Fisher and Jemima Puddle-
Duck. And their creator still lived and had her being, right there!
The glimpse of that house intrigued me far more than did the homes
of Wordsworth and Ruskin which we had seen earlier. I said: 'If I
only had a copy of one of her books, I'd almost be tempted to knock
on her door and beg her to autograph it.'

My hostess looked thoughtful. 'I think Mrs Heelis might be very interested in meeting a member of the Canadian Air Force who remembered her books. When we get home I'll give her a ring. We might find one of her books for you in Kendal.'

And that is how it happened that two days later I found myself on my way to meet the creator of Peter Rabbit.

It was snowy that day, I remember, and while we were still stamping our feet on the porch the door opened. I think I must have been expecting a wispy, poetic sort of person, but the woman who greeted us was a stocky little lady in the late seventies, very stooped, her hands and feet gnarled and misshapen from rheumatism, but with a smiling, red-cheeked face and a pair of the shrewdest sparkling eyes I ever saw. She looked exactly like a very sensible sort of grandmother. And to my delight she wore a frilled white cap with a lace edge, something I had not seen on anyone's head since my own grandmother died about the time I was growing out of the Peter Rabbit books.

She welcomed us cordially and took us into a comfortable farmhouse parlor where there were boxes piled on chairs, a heap of curtain material on a table, and a large framed picture standing with its face to the wall. For a few minutes she devoted herself to my hostess, and they exchanged some talk about Girl Guide work. Then, with a smile, Mrs Heelis turned to me and asked what part of Canada I came from.

During the war I learned to dread that polite question, for then I had usually to face some further remark like: 'Oh, yes, I've heard Ontario is a very beautiful city.' This time I need not have worried. What part of Ontario? Grey County. Was that anywhere near the St Lawrence? No; I explained its location. Was it mainly a rural county? Yes, it was, and I told her quite a bit about it.

'The reason I know a little about Ontario,' she said, 'is that my husband and I considered emigrating there after the First World War, and we even decided where we would settle – it was on the St Lawrence below Lake Ontario. Then a big property here in Westmorland came on the market, and after hesitating, we decided to buy it and stay where we are.'

So Canada lost the creator of Peter Rabbit as a citizen . . .

'I brought this out in case you might be interested,' said Mrs Heelis, and she handed me the picture that I had noticed standing by the wall. And I nearly dropped it, for there in my hand were all the original pictures for Peter Rabbit, set out as a panel and framed as a whole – bright little watercolors, just a little bigger than the reproductions that we know in the books. Peter squeezing under the gate, sitting at ease eating radishes, caught in the gooseberry net – with the sparrows 'imploring him to

exert himself' – and all the rest of them. It was an odd feeling to hold the originals of pictures that had been reproduced well over a million times, and absorbed by how many million pairs of small eyes?

I had two of her books for Mrs Heelis to autograph – *Mrs. Tittlemouse* and *Benjamin Bunny*. You may recall that the London blitz destroyed most of the publishers' stocks and, as few books could be reprinted while the war lasted, it was pure luck to find these copies. Mrs Heelis flipped through them in a businesslike way.

'Not bad,' she said, examining the colors critically. 'Some editions have been a disgrace – these are not bad.'

Then with a scratchy steel pen she inscribed the title page of each of them with my name and the words: 'With kind regards from Beatrix Potter, May 10th, 1943.' And do you think any dear little kiddies have been allowed to lay their paws on these two copies since I brought them home? Not likely!

That was in May. Beatrix Potter died in December of that same year, leaving a great fortune. Much of it was in land – in fact I believe she died the largest single landowner in the Lake District – and all was left to the National Trust. I did not know till I read her biography later that she was not born there, but was a London child of wealthy parents who gave her an upbringing in unbending Victorian style. She was in her forties before she burst her bonds and turned with a sigh of content into the countrywoman, Mrs Heelis.

There is one more thing that sticks in my mind. When we left, we took a shortcut back of the cottage, and I noticed some hutches containing several of Peter's cousins. It would be nice to think they were kept as pets, but I am afraid it is just a pious hope. During the meat rationing of the last war, the British Government encouraged people to raise meat in their own back yards to eke out the ration. And apart from poultry the best little back-yard meat producers are rabbits. I am afraid it is pretty certain that each of those rabbits was going to be put into a pie, not by the terrible Mr McGregor, but by Beatrix Potter herself.

*It was in 1935 that Josephine and Delmar Banner first met Beatrix
Potter. They were young artists, she a sculptor and he a painter, who
for many years had been visiting the Lake District for their holidays,
staying and working on farms while they searched for a house in which
to settle permanently. Having been admirers of Beatrix Potter's work
for a long time, they were delighted when a farmer friend arranged for
them to meet her. It was the start of a close friendship.
Following Beatrix Potter's death on 22 December 1943 Delmar
Banner wrote a number of articles about her, including 'An
Appreciation' in* The Times *of 30 December. The following piece
was published in the October 1946 issue of* The Nineteenth
Century and After, *a monthly review founded in 1877 and later
called* The Twentieth Century.
*After her death Delmar Banner made two portraits in oils of Beatrix
Potter, one from an early photograph and the other from his
remarkable visual memory. The later picture, 'Beatrix Potter in Old
Age' (see opposite), depicts her at an agricultural show, with the
Lakeland fells in the background. It was presented by the artist to the
National Portrait Gallery in London in 1948.*

MEMORIES OF BEATRIX POTTER

DELMAR BANNER, 1946

When a stranger comes into a Lakeland Cottage, Something,
diffused through the room as the air itself, recedes into the
shadows; watching and hiding there till the new presence has
gone. The Stranger knows it will never come out while he is
there – even if the old folk move out, and he takes their place,
living there till his footsteps have worn the door-sill lower – it
will only emerge when he is in bed. If he comes down in the night

there is a cool smell, distinct, but neither sweet nor acid – and he knows that the Past is out and alive in the old house. It is not unfriendly, only still, and 'candlewise'. This same 'withdrawing' is present in a meeting between an 'offcome' and a native of the Dales. A silence, a searching gaze; weighing and sounding. Thus it was at our first meeting with Mrs Heelis. (From a letter from Josephine Banner to Margaret Lane.)

We had the privilege of her friendship: though she was older than our parents. Many have failed to meet her. She refused to be lionized. She did not 'call' on newcomers; she sometimes went to the back door with a sack over her shoulders, and judged by her reception there. She was busy: she disliked contacts and novelty.

We were introduced by a farmer; almost the only way. She fixed a time: we knocked on the door of her cottage one autumn afternoon. It opened, and we beheld one of her own characters – Mrs Tiggy-winkle perhaps? – yet better than any; short, plump, solid; with apple-red cheeks; and she looked up at us with keen blue eyes and a smile. On her head was a kind of tea-cosy, and she was dressed in lots of wool. 'Cum in,' she said in a snug voice. There was drugget on the floor, and silver-mounted guns on the wall. In the room into which we followed her bent and venerable figure there was a cheerful fire. She sat down on a red plush armchair on one side, and we sat on stiff-backed chairs on the other. She took us in; and during that searching silence we neither spoke nor moved. We noticed a fine Girtin on the wall; her husband's slippers warming on the fender; and (for her age) a rather naughty quantity of silver chocolate-paper on a little table.

Like the true northerner she had become, she took her time, but eventually she was chuckling and patting her knees, as she did when pleased; and in the end she raised her plump hands and slapped her short lap, indulging in little rolls as she laughed. She approved of us for being Cumbrians; and for working, and for not being in a hurry. ('Eh lad, never be in a hurry,' said the Coniston shoemaker (a pupil of Ruskin's) to me: and we once asked a farmer here in Little Langdale the name of his horse, and he replied, 'We haven't given 'un a name yet: we've nobbut had 'un a twelvemonth.')

The next day, to our astonishment, she came to see us, at Hawkshead, where we were staying. She was friendly, though, as usual, downright. We told her we had not yet found a home in the dales for our work; she looked thoughtful, and said 'I've some labourers' cottages, but I'll not let you have one of them.' I asked her to sign the petition against afforestation in Eskdale: she refused; she had not gone into it thoroughly; also (I fear) there had been a dispute with one of its promoters, over a bull. She looked at my pictures, made sound criticism, and bought one. When we saw her off, she turned at the gate, grinned at us, and said, 'I'll do all I can for you: I don't know why: I don't know anything about you: but I've taken to you.'

Next summer we saw her again several times: and so each year. At the Eskdale sheep show she looked the real sheep breeder, and rosier than ever. A farmer slapped her on the back, and she talked of 'John Peel when he'd had a couple'. But the dalesmen are never 'familiar' and she was profoundly respected. Besides, one farmer said to us, 'It won't do to tread on yon lass's corns.' And she knew her job. Dr Milne, of Newcastle Agricultural College, gave us a long account of her knowledge of sheep diseases.

In the morning she was solidly at business: she had told us not to speak to her till the afternoon – she would have been very short with us if we had; but when we went up to her beside the pen containing her prize 'yows', she beamed up at us with her countenance full of intelligence and humour, in which all that is most direct, dignified and engaging in childhood and age seemed to meet. It was there that we first met her husband; a typical country lawyer.

She invited us to lunch. She asked us not to 'tease' her husband, if he came, about cottages. We asked if she would show us the original drawings for the illustrations in her books; works of art as perfect as the stories. She said: 'Aye: I keep them behind the geyser'; and toddled off. We heard the creaking of the stairs as she climbed slowly up, and then, after an interval of little noises, down again, armed with bundles in brown paper, fastened with blue ribbon. We saw how exquisite – beyond our hopes and beyond the means of colour-reproduction – the pictures are. She told us the outlines, which seem to us to strengthen, were not in the first drawings, and remained a distasteful convention to her, but were advised by the printers. She identified all the places; every scene can be found, mostly near Sawrey and Hawkshead; some  further off, like those in *Mrs. Tiggy-Winkle* in Newlands; and Pigling and Pig-wig Bland go to live in Little Langdale; it is Colwith Bridge that they 'crossed hand in hand' (like a human pair – one of whom Mrs Heelis afterwards always called 'Pig-wig'). She said 'I can't invent: I only copy.' (Like Leonardo.) Yet nothing could be more invented. (The romantic modern word 'create' is one she disliked, as cant and not true: God 'creates': man invents.) This exactness and moderation is significant.

She had a perfect sense of fitness for incidentals. The Foxy-whiskered Gentleman is no longer dressed when he peeps at Jemima's eggs – it adds much to his villainy. Jemima does not wear her ridiculous costume when she has achieved her ducklings; that gives her back her natural beauty and dignity. (From a letter from Josephine Banner to Margaret Lane.)

Another year she led us over the field from her full little garden to Hill Top Farm, where she had once lived, and where some visitors were still entertained under the delusion that she occupied it: she concealed her real burrow. She had the love of secrecy which belongs to the little creatures of the woods.

Hill Top (now a museum in her memory) retains the furniture and fittings that she painted, with the enchantment that only naturalism can distil, in *Tom Kitten*, *Samuel Whiskers*, and other books: the door at which Tabitha welcomed her guests, the chimney up which Tom climbed, the staircase up which Mrs Whiskers ran with provisions: the windows, beds and dresser: and the chair on which sat a 'perfectly beautiful [lovely] little [black] Berkshire pig'.

Her realism and grasp of how things worked underlay her imaginative freedom (as it always does). It was in her unpedantic technical finish, her undistorted specific observation: it went to lengths to astonish the romantic nature-scorner: for she told us, 'I articulated skeletons with my brothers: we once boiled a Fox. The smell was dreadful.' She knew Mr Tod at close quarters.

But when we spoke of admiration for her art she only said, thoughtfully, half to herself, 'Aye, they'll do nobody any harm.'

We noticed her respect for her husband. But for him she would probably have been more naughty than she was – for although she always seemed warmly dressed, it was surely naughty to work in the hayfield at seventy-six with a truss (and have to lie down in it in consequence): and surely naughty to scramble out of bed in her last illness and go into the autumn garden (even though in her husband's greatcoat and three pairs of knickers) to pull up the last cabbage, because she saw it from her window being eaten by slugs.

I believe she regarded it as not only her duty, but her right, to preserve old houses: indeed, she wrote to us 'Captain Kettle dances the hornpipe by himself!' No one did it better: and no one ever bequeathed a grander gift to the National Trust. But she was glad when we got our home in Little Langdale.

It was not till middle life that the success of her books freed her to live in Sawrey. But she loved the fells and their people; and belonged, truly, to this 'Natural Republic' – as Wordsworth called it.

I am sure she often thought in the dialect, and certainly spoke it to farmers. She was 'one of us', though such a personality was bound to find opposition from a few. One of these went out of his way to try to prevent her from getting some property. She said 'Old --- and I are waiting for each other to die!' – then chuckled. One was reminded of the interior of Mr Tod's house, where the last plate of old Vixen Tod always sends a cold shiver down one's marrow as it cracks on the bare flags. One would expect her (from her books) to have realism and humour, but she was so fresh and varied that one often had surprises. And the tinge of grimness was of the North. Other people seemed less real, and their talk like a string of half-remembered clichés, after hers. (From a letter from Josephine Banner to Margaret Lane.)

To us, three things seem to mark the end of an age in the Cumbrian dales. One, the flooding of Mardale; one the invasion of the motor; and one the passing of Mrs Heelis. And at her death a young shepherd said to us, 'Aye, it's a bad day for farmers.'

The last time my wife ever saw her was in August 1943. She went with our two boys. Mrs Tiggy-Winkle was very bent, and confessed her escapade in the hayfield. She was more snug than ever. When my wife left, Mrs Tiggy leant on the little gate with her head on one side, smiling and waving goodbye with a clover-leaf – the same gate from which Timmy Willie had waved his daisy.

In October 1942 The Times Literary Supplement *published the first of a series that was to appear regularly for the next two and a half years. The pieces were full-page critical essays and anonymous, bearing only the by-line 'Menander's Mirror'. The style was mellow and meditative and the subjects varied from empty pews in churches to the permissive society. The identity of the author was widely discussed and there were many who shrewdly (and correctly) guessed that the writer was Charles Morgan. His tribute to Beatrix Potter appeared on 8 January 1944, seventeen days after her death.*

THE TAILOR OF GLOUCESTER

CHARLES MORGAN, MENANDER'S MIRROR, 1944

THE DISADVANTAGE OF Beatrix Potter's books is not so much that, like other books, they are lost or synonymously borrowed, as that they wear out. This is through no fault of the binders and papermakers or of the publishers, Messrs Warne, all of whom have done their duty. Nothing short of vellum and a chain could protect the Potter books from the ravages of youth. Even the two Alices are safer, though, heaven knows, they are read as much; and they are safer for two reasons: that the Elders of the Household claim a semi-proprietary and so a protective right in them, and that they are larger. In the nursery, no one can ever be sure that Alice belongs to him and to him alone, to do what he will with. Elders take a serious interest in her; they quote her as they quote Shakespeare (and much oftener); they carry her off into libraries and drawing-rooms and expect her to have a clean face and, in general, a neat appearance. No one makes any such solemn or polite demands of the Potter books.

They are nursery books, and, when Elders steal them, it is

stealing. They belong to the nursery without division of ownership; they are your own there, to do your best or your worst with; and, when they begin to disintegrate, you mend them, or forget to mend them, with sticky paper. That is one reason for their glorious impermanence. The other is that they are so many and so small – so many that, if one should vanish, all you have to do is to close up the ranks and wait for reinforcements; so small that, unlike the more dignified Alice, they get into the most astonishing places, they retreat from the pillow to the bed, they slide down between the sheets and can be slept on without discomfort, they will fit into any pocket and are good mixers with whatever alive or glutinous may have accumulated there, and, again unlike Alice who has always one eye on her privilege as a drawing-room classic, they acquire great charm from scars and bandages. She, too, matures with age, but in the manner of a vintage – that is to say, sedately, for she was always a sedate little girl. But the Potter books thrive upon hard treatment. They can be used as literature, as projectiles or as bricks. Moreover, if you can read anything on earth, you can read them unaided. They are on the pillow or the hearthrug almost as soon as your mind takes cognizance of literature's original and fundamental truth: that the Cat is on the Mat. And they go on for years. Many a time it has been with the Potter books that Balbus has built his wall.

It is, therefore, not surprising that the ancient Balbus, hearing with sadness of Beatrix Potter's death, should leave the attic in which now he himself writes books that the nursery would scorn, and find his way downstairs to the room in which her works hold their place. The room itself has been perverted from its former use, but the forms have been preserved. The cupboards and doors still have china handles painted with roses, and inside the cupboards a yellow locomotive of the old Brighton Railway still waits patiently until someone shall be young and brave enough to raise steam in her boiler. Within their cardboard boxes the Household Cavalry cara-cole and piaffe in face of the enemy, and near by is a dictionary for those who need it. On the walls hangs a tinted engraving of Frith's *Derby Day*; and the books are still the same books – Stevenson,

Ballantyne, *De Bello Gallico*, Lang, George Macdonald, and, on the third shelf of the right-hand bookcase, the Potter-bricks of Balbus's first wall.

But how they are diminished! How many years have passed since any gap was filled! Now at last one understands the argument of those who wish to increase the birth-rate . . .. Still, there they are, the survivors, splendid in bandages – enough, says Balbus to himself as he spreads them out before the fireguard, to annihilate

Germany for an hour and put back the hands of the clock. He looks at once for the leaders: Peter Rabbit, for example; and Nutkin who 'had a brother called Twinkleberry, and a great many cousins'; and the disagreeable Mr Tod. Yes, but where is *The Tailor of Gloucester*? In another shelf, perhaps, strayed from his companions? Or in another room, it may be, captured years ago and long held prisoner. Not in the house? Out into the streets, then! Visit the booksellers. North, south, east, west – where is *The Tailor of Gloucester*? He does not answer to his name; and there, spread out before the fireguard, are his brothers, waiting for him. Balbus, returned, a little ashamed of having neglected them so long, sits down upon the hearthrug to meditate.

It is a solemn thought that, if we could know certainly why the Potter books are held in such warm regard, we should be able to make a valuable contribution to the work of the psychologists – not of child-psychologists only but of national psychologists as well. For example, it is clear that one of their peculiarities, when they began to come out, was that they were amoral and non-educational. It is a fair guess that to the English this was a recommendation. Every German knows that we are a frivolous people, 'incapable of reflection,' as Goethe said, and though, during the nineteenth century, Kingsley and his brethren had tagged a moral to every tale, we had, in the early years of Edward VII, reverted to type. But what of Scotland? Not even a German philosopher could say that the Scots are incapable of reflection or that they dislike being educated. Were the Potter books less readily accepted north of the Tweed than among the frivolous and unreflecting children of the South? What has been their fortune in France, in Scandinavia, in Germany itself? Given the statistics, the psychologists could prove everything with them. 'The Political and Racial Implications of Peter Rabbit and his Tribe, considered in their Relationship to the Doctrines of Spengler' might come from Heidelberg. A thesis from Yale 'On Samuel Whiskers and the Problem of Imperialism' might bear as its epigraph:

Once upon a time there was an old cat, called Mrs Tabitha Twitchit, who was an anxious parent. She used to lose her kittens continually, and whenever they were lost they were always in mischief!

Only a Frenchman can tell what conclusions might be drawn at the Sorbonne from a close study of the English mind's response to

the works of Beatrix Potter. It would seem to him a strangely irrational and inconsequent mind. He would quote little Benjamin's remark – 'It spoils people's clothes to squeeze under a gate; the proper way to get in, is to climb down a pear tree.' – and would observe with astonishment that, to the English, this appeared to make sense. What sense does it make, he would ask, except the plainest, the commonest sense? What is the element of wit contained in it that makes an Englishman smile when he reads it? And why are the English so helplessly inarticulate on the subject of their own wit and humour? Even when they are articulate, their theory seems to have no correspondence with their practice. Sydney Smith said:

> The relation discovered [by wit] must be something remote from all the common tracks and sheep-walks made in the mind; it must not be a comparison of colour with colour, and figure with figure, or any comparison which, though individually new, is specifically stale . . . but it must be something removed from common apprehension, distant from the ordinary haunts of thought . . .

Yes, yes the Frenchman would reply, that may explain in advance the devotion of the English to Lewis Carroll. It amuses them to perceive a relationship between two things wildly incongruous, and all Europe knows the infuriating and irrelevant smile which, in battle or at the council-table, dawns in the face of an Englishman when he has seen a joke of this kind. It may be called the Smile of the Snark. But there is another, the Seraphic Grin, which neither Sydney Smith nor anyone alive or dead has ever explained. Quote that piece about the gate and the pear tree; the Seraphic Grin will almost certainly welcome it. Why? Can it be because it is concerned with rabbits, and rabbits do not wear clothes? Can it be because a coat is torn as easily by climbing down a pear tree as by squeezing under a gate? Ask an Englishman these questions and he will shake his head – and smile again. What is the answer?

We know; but it is true that we cannot tell. We are bound to leave the racial, political and statistical implications of Peter Rabbit to Heidelberg, and the theory of British humour to Paris. All we can say is that the Potter books are not deliberately humorous, and point out to the French, who are aware of Flaubert's theory, that one of their merits is that they are factual. They tell you what was done and said, and leave you to draw your own moral or romantic conclusions. Consider this:

Although it was midnight, Pécuchet fancied a turn in the garden. Bouvard had no objection. They took the candle, and shading it with an old newspaper walked round the borders. It was a pleasure to name the vegetables. 'Look – the carrots! And cabbages!'

And hear the echo:

Peter said he thought he might feel better if he went for a walk. They went away hand in hand, and got upon the flat top of the wall at the bottom of the wood.

And, after they had reached the garden (by way of the factual pear tree):

Then he suggested that they should fill the pocket-handkerchief with onions, as a little present for his Aunt.

Peter did not seem to be enjoying himself; he kept hearing noises.

Benjamin, on the contrary, was perfectly at home, and ate a lettuce leaf. He said that he was in the habit of coming to the garden with his father to get lettuces for their Sunday dinner.

Bouvard and Pécuchet is so remarkable an exercise of genius that there have been critics who, for the sake of its carefully dried factualism, have set it before even *Madame Bovary*, which has seemed to them, by comparison, lush. They have worshipped *Bouvard and Pécuchet* much less for its virtue of implicit feeling than for its mannerism of restraint – a mannerism which chimed with their own impotence and seemed to justify their inability to let themselves go. What they could not do, they praised Flaubert for having deliberately refrained from doing, as though a boiler without steam in it should say that the whole art of engineering consisted in refusing to allow the pressure to rise. When you are a master of prose, as Flaubert was, it is dangerous to reject four-fifths of its opportunities – dangerous to others, if not to yourself. Apart from all else, it is extremely misleading to the coteries. They assume at once that the dry, factual style, which you, the great Flaubert, apply to the special instance of *Bouvard and Pécuchet*, is applicable to all novels, and begin at once to think less of, disparage, shall we say Gautier, for not having applied it to *Mademoiselle de Maupin*. What they fail to notice is how near Flaubert's style, in *Bouvard and Pécuchet*, came sometimes to prattling. Translate it into English, put a passage from Beatrix Potter beside it, and, behold, Peter Rabbit and Benjamin Bunny emerge as a critical pastiche of Bouvard and Pécuchet.

Conversely, the comparison, because it is fantastic and, as Sydney Smith said, 'distant from the ordinary haunts of thought', may throw light on Peter Rabbit's authority over the hearthrug. Beatrix Potter was applying a factual style to children's fantasy, and, in the same sphere, this had not been done before. Other writers were either too elaborate or too moral or too facetious or too hearty or too grotesque. Beatrix Potter was never grotesque. In a period when ugliness, brutality and distortion were becoming as fashionable in the toyshops as among the picture-dealers, the illustrations to her books relied for their effect upon none of these things, nor even upon farce. Farce, at its lowest, is for tired tradesmen; at a slightly higher level, for the braying-sort who rejoice in the humiliation of the human animal. On rare occasions of genius something at root farcical undergoes an enchantment and becomes a masterpiece, but the rule of farcical damnation stands. The Potter illustrations eluded it. They had, even, the courage to be pretty, which, at a time when it was considered funny to draw a kitten as if it were a gargoyle, was in itself a bold defiance of the commercial rule, and there are probably many readers who, if asked why these books were loved, would give as their reason the marine procession of squirrels crossing to Owl Island on rafts of twigs or the picture of the mouse, who escaped from Miss Moppet, 'dancing a jig on the top of the cupboard!' But, admirable though the illustrations are, their virtue is what the virtue of an illustration always is, that they fulfil the text, and, though the text pretends sometimes to be scarcely more than a 'caption' to the pictures, we must not be deceived into heresy. The virtue is in the story. We must find it there.

The rule obeyed is the old one; a beginning, a middle, an end: an illusion sufficient to maintain suspense of plot; a good humour warm enough to yield the pleasures of good company. Beatrix Potter had, too, the gift of attack. Without preliminary atmospherics, she plunged into narrative.

> One morning a little rabbit sat on a bank.
> He pricked his ears and listened to
> the trit-trot, trit-trot of a pony.
> A gig was coming along the road;
> it was driven by Mr McGregor, and
> beside him sat Mrs McGregor in
> her best bonnet.
> As soon as they had passed . . .

Goldsmith could not have opened more plainly or Stevenson have wasted less time. And observe the unforced simplicity of the endings. There is no rumbling of final chords, no hesitation in 'sitting down'. When you have said what you have to say, you stop, like this:

> When Peter got home, his mother forgave him, because she was so glad to see that he had found his shoes and coat. Cotton-tail and Peter folded up the pocket-handkerchief, and old Mrs Rabbit strung up the onions and hung them from the kitchen ceiling, with the bunches of herbs and the rabbit-tobacco.

The effect of this method upon you, when you were very young, was the same as the effect of Lang's *Blue Fairy Book*, or of Stevenson's *Treasure Island* when you were older – that of making you feel that the story-teller seriously believed in his own story and, for that reason, was imparting it. The Potter books, in brief, though the composition of them may have been as elaborate as Stevenson's, give an impression, not, indeed, of casualness, but of unself-consciousness – above all of freedom from that particular bending selfconsciousness, that pawky rib-digging slyness, which, whether with a moral or commercial purpose, deliberately supplies what is called the 'juvenile market'. It is the plain honesty of their story-telling and the fact that, on however small a scale, they have a story to tell, which has always tempted Balbus to read these bricks in the wall. He reads them still. But where *is The Tailor of Gloucester*?

Two generations of children had been brought up on the little books before anything at all was known about their author, for Beatrix Potter was strongly averse to publicity and refused all requests for interviews. It was Margaret Lane's biography, The Tale of Beatrix Potter, *that in 1946 first told the world about this remarkable woman and which prompted the research and investigation into every detail of her life and work that has continued ever since. Margaret Lane's account of what she called 'her brush with the memory of Beatrix Potter' was first published in* Punch *on 14 November 1962, in a series entitled 'Children's Classics Revisited', and reprinted four years later in a collection of her essays,* Purely for Pleasure *(Hamish Hamilton, 1966). Other articles in the 'Children's Classics Revisited' series included Siriol Hugh Jones on* Alice *and J. B. Priestley on* Five Children and It.

THE GHOST OF BEATRIX POTTER

MARGARET LANE, 1962

MOST OF THE hallowed books of childhood lose something of their magic as we grow older. Beatrix Potter's never. She even, to the mature eye, reveals felicities and depths of irony which pass the childish reader by; the dewy freshness of her landscape recalls Constable; her animals, for all the anthropomorphism of their dress and behaviour, show an imaginative fidelity to nature, a microscopic truth that one finds in the hedgerow woodcuts of Thomas Bewick.

It would be unwise to say any of this if she were still alive. She died in 1943, her brief creative period (thirteen years in all) having come to a close some thirty years before, since when she had evolved into a rather crusty and intimidating person, interested mainly in acquiring land and breeding Herdwick sheep, and whom nothing annoyed more than to have her books appraised on a critical level. . . .

I could, if asked, have warned anybody that it was unwise to meddle at all with Beatrix Potter, having nearly done so myself in 1939, when I was very sharply sent about my business. Like most people who have been wholly entranced by her little books in infancy, I had long believed that Beatrix Potter was dead. The occasional new production that one came across in bookshops (*A Fierce Bad Rabbit*, for example) was so egregiously bad compared with the early masterpieces as to strengthen the suspicion that they were written by somebody else. The bookshops denied this, and were not believed. It was no good asking questions about Beatrix Potter, because at that time nobody knew anything about her.

It was in the early days of the war that I first discovered that she was still alive, and living in the Lake District. My stepdaughter was at school near Windermere, and brought home tempting scraps of some local legends that were current about her. She was very old. She was very rich. She was a recluse. She was a little mad. She drove round the lake on Sundays in an open carriage, wearing black lace and sitting very stiffly behind the coachman. (This, it turned out, was a memory of her mother, Mrs Rupert Potter, who had done exactly that.) Or alternatively, and this was the most popular legend of all, she did labourer's work in the fields, wearing sacks and rags.

It was very puzzling, but at least it seemed undeniable that she was still alive, and I fell, like Graham Greene and Miss Adam Smith soon after, into the innocent folly of wishing to write about her. Clearly, if she were as reclusive as people said, one must approach with care, and since it seemed desirable to go to the fountain-head as a precaution against inaccuracy or offence, I decided to write to her.

The sensible approach, indeed the only one, since I did not know where she lived, was through her publishers, and I wrote to Frederick Warne and Co. for her address. They replied with ill-concealed horror that on no account, in no possible circumstances, could her address be given. She lived in close retirement, she never saw anybody, they had her express instructions that nobody must ever be allowed to write her a letter.

This could have been final, but it was also rather a challenge to ingenuity, and since my intentions were of the most serious and respectful description I could not see why they should refuse to forward a letter. They did not refuse, though they clearly shrank from the impertinence, and in due course an extremely polite missive was forwarded to Sawrey. I told her of my lifelong pleasure in her books (addressing her, I am thankful to remember, as Mrs Heelis), expressed my admiration and my wish to write an essay on her work, and asked if I might one day call on her to check some facts and submit what I should write for her approval.

Back came, in a few days, the rudest letter I have ever received in my life. Certainly not, she said; nothing would induce her to see me. 'My books have always sold without advertisement, and I do not propose to go in for that sort of thing now.' Her reply could hardly have been more offensively worded if I had asked her to sponsor a deodorant advertisement.

Well, that was that, I thought. It would be impossible to write anything in the face of such hostility, a snub so out of proportion to the occasion. I tore up the letter in indignation, not knowing that I was only one of innumerable people who had had the breath knocked out of them by her acerbity.

And then, in 1943, she died; and Raymond Mortimer, at that time literary editor of *The New Statesman*, asked if I could write him an article on Beatrix Potter. I did my best, but it was a poor best, for nobody seemed to know anything about her and the crumbs of fact I could gather were contemptible. I knew only that she had lived and farmed for years in the Lake District and was the wife of a country solicitor. I had to confine myself to an appreciation of her work, and even this contained some sad inaccuracies.

It soon became apparent, from the meagre obituary notices which followed, that I was not the only one who had failed to find out anything. The tone, everywhere, was one of surprise that she had been so recently alive, and it was suddenly borne in on me that what

I wanted to do was to write her biography. Alas for such optimism! Here was a life so innocent, so uneventful that one would have supposed the only difficulty would be in finding something to say. Yet, when I approached her widower, the gentlest of men, who received me with a trembling blend of terror and courtesy, it appeared that he considered himself under oath to conceal the very few facts that he had in his possession. He knew remarkably little about her life before their marriage, which had taken place when she was approaching fifty. He impressed me as a man who for thirty years had lived under the rule of a fairly dominant feminine authority, and whenever, reluctantly, he imparted a scrap of information or a date, he would glance apprehensively over his shoulder, as though every moment expecting the door to open.

The house was indeed palpably haunted by her. She had not long been dead, and the imprint of her personality, clearly the more dynamic one in that marriage, was on every chair and table. Her clothes still hung behind the door, her geraniums trailed and bloomed along the window-sill, her muddles lay unsorted at one end of the table while he took his meals at the other, even a half-eaten bar of chocolate with her teeth-marks in it lay whitened and stale among the litter of letters on her writing-table.

Yet he had expressed himself willing, after much patient argument, that a biography should be written, and as a man of honour truly believed that he was doing his best. He had been, it is true, quite implacable at first, and had been at pains to explain, with the most considerate politeness, why such a project was impossible. She would not have wished it, he said; what was more, she would never have allowed it; and here he looked over his shoulder again and blew his nose in a large and dubious handkerchief. The argument which finally convinced him, in spite of his obvious misgiving that agreement was treachery, was that sooner or later, either in England or America, a biography would be written, and it was perhaps better to have it written while he was still alive and could presumably exercise some control over the biographer. He seemed relieved to think that by this means he might escape the attentions of some frantic American, but I had to promise that every word of every line should be subject to his inspection, and left the cottage after that first interview with my point gained, in the deepest possible dejection.

I knew exactly what he had in mind; the sort of biography he had at last brought himself, after the most scrupulous searching of conscience, to consider. It would be about a quarter of an inch thick, bound in navy blue boards with gilt lettering, and would be called *A Memoir of the late Mrs William Heelis.* We did not discuss the point, but I am sure he took it for granted that it would be for private circulation.

Then began a series of evenings which we spent together and which I look back on with misery. Every question, however innocuous, was met with the frightened response, 'Oh, you can't mention *that!*' Any detail of her parents, the date of her birth, even the fact of her marriage to himself fell under this extraordinary prohibition. Night after night I stretched my tact and ingenuity to breaking-point, feverishly changing from subject to subject, retreating at once when I saw his poor eyes watering in alarm, creeping back each night to my cold bedroom at the Sawrey inn to sleepless hours of knowing the whole thing to be impossible.

And then, after many evenings and by the merest accident, I changed my tune. Some tremulous negative, some futile protest over a harmless question, produced that sudden trembling which I have experienced only two or three times in my life and associate with the crisis known as losing one's temper. I found myself banging the table with clenched fist and crying 'Mr Heelis, you *must not obstruct me in this way!*' The moment it had happened, in the petrified silence, I was overcome with embarrassment. But the effect was magical. He jumped, looked over his shoulder again as towards a voice he knew, pulled himself together, blew his nose, apologized, and suddenly seemed to feel remarkably better. I had never meant to do it, but the inference was plain. Tact, compliance, the yielding deviousness that had cost me so much effort, were things he was unaccustomed to and could not deal with. With decision, with firm opinion, he felt at home, and responded in the most eager and obliging manner. Pleased at last to be able to express his pride in his wife's fame he brought out his boxes of letters, rummaged in the bottoms of wardrobes and at the backs of drawers for photographs, produced such addresses and names as from time to time crossed his uncertain memory. The thing was started; I breathed a sigh of relief; though not without foreboding that my difficulties were only begun.

They were indeed, for over his eager compliance, which even extended to giving me two of her watercolours, hung the cloud of that final inspection of the manuscript which I knew would mar all. Left to himself, with typescript before him, I knew how his trembling hand would score it through, how little, how very little would come back unscathed, how in despair I would fling that little into the wastepaper basket.

Outside the precincts of Castle Cottage there was no such reticence; there were many people living who had known her well, Potter cousins, the niece of her last governess, Miss Hammond, innumerable farm and cottage neighbours who thought of her only as the eccentric little figure that the Lake District remembers – the odd bundle of country clothing, clad in innumerable petticoats, full of good humour, of authority, of sudden acerbities which would flash out quite brutally and inflict hurts where she probably never intended them. 'I began to assert myself at seventy', she wrote to one of her cousins a few months before she died, but this was an understatement. She had been asserting herself for thirty years, and the Lake District had come to respect her as a person it was dangerous to oppose, but very safe to love.

Those who spoke of her with the most feeling were the shepherds and farmers with whom she was most akin in temperament, and to the poetry of whose lives she had always responded, almost with the nostalgia of an exile. On her deathbed she had scribbled a note of indecipherable farewell to her old Scottish shepherd, the 'lambing-time man' who had come to her every spring for nearly twenty years, and with whom she had kept up a long and affectionate correspondence. He had preserved all her letters, dated and wrapped up in little parcels in the recesses of his cottage, and he sent them to me as an act of piety, for love of her memory.

I took innumerable journeys, sometimes with Mr Heelis, more often (and more fruitfully) alone, over the fells and along the valleys, to cottages and farmhouses that she owned, talking to the people who had known her. She had been a workmanlike landlord, most practically interested in fences and gates, the felling and planting of timber, the repairing of walls. As a sheep breeder she

was knowledgeable and shrewd, and the farmers round about thought of her principally as a dangerous rival at sheep fairs and ram shows, an enigmatic and authoritative presence in the Keswick tavern where the Herdwick Sheep Breeders' Association held its meetings.

At the same time I embarked on a sea of correspondence, which ebbed and flowed for more than a year. Beatrix Potter, for all the crowded busyness of her later years, when she was managing a number of farms and doing important work for the National Trust in the Lake District, possessed that last-century sense of leisure which permitted her to write long and frequent letters to a great many people – sometimes even to people she had never met, but whose personalities, when they wrote to her, had taken her fancy.

Now, these letters began to flow into my hands, not only from English senders, but from places as far afield as America and New Zealand; and the task of deciphering and sifting them for their shreds of biographical interest was for a time quite heavy.

To me, the series of letters which Warne, her publishers for more than forty years, had kept without a gap since the day when they first accepted *Peter Rabbit*, was the most interesting of all, for they reflected her slow and painstaking development as an artist, her emotional growth from girl to woman, her emergence from unhappy and respectable nonentity into the kind of personality about whom biographies are written. The Warne family had played an important, and more than professional, part in her life, and without their help and confidence the book could never have been written.

But however much help I had from her publishers, relations and other friends, there was still to be faced the final confrontation with Mr Heelis, when, as I privately guessed, he would bring up reinforcements of prohibition and his mandate would fall on everything I had written.

I remember that on my last evening at Sawrey, returning from a walk with which I had tried in vain to recruit my spirits, I found a penny lying at the foot of a stile and decided to toss for it; whether I should give it up there and then or write the book as I saw it and be prepared to forget it for years in a locked drawer. The penny said heads, and I put it in my pocket as a charm. The drawer was the thing. I did not know how old Mr Heelis was, nor how I should explain my curious delay; but I was resolved I would not expose myself, or him, to the long-drawn agony of his excisions.

As it turned out, the penny proved a true oracle, for the poor widower, left alone and at a loss without the mainstay on which his thoughts and decisions had so long depended, died a few months after, before the book was finished, and I never paid that final visit to Sawrey. I do not believe he turns in his grave, honest man, nor that the stout little ghost which haunts the place would still, after all this time, find it necessary to be angry.

ane Moore's article was first published on 9 February 1946 in
Time and Tide: *'An Independent Non-Party Weekly Review'*
which was founded in 1920 and which ceased publication in 1977.

CRIME IN BEATRIX POTTER

JANE MOORE, 1946

THERE IS NO pandering to parental conventions when Beatrix Potter writes for her chosen public. Long words are not ruled out if the occasion requires them, neither are hard facts glossed over. For it is a mirror of life, a complete and satisfying world which that public demands and they already know that life has its seamy side which no politeness can veil or parents altogether avert. Nor would most of them have it otherwise. The exquisite safety of early morning sunshine in the nursery were nothing without the shadows of the night before, and the reassurance of such masterpieces as *Mrs. Tiggy-Winkle* should be set off by contrasting depths of mystery and crime.

Besides, there is a fascination in crime on its own account. If the humours of Sherlock Holmes with his Watson, against an irresistibly murky background or the paradoxical pieties of Father Brown, or the surprising accomplishments of Lord Peter, or the debonair M. Poirot, or the inexorable Maigret or any other idols of detection, leave us cold, we are perhaps to be stirred by some brisk celluloid shooting from the States or a verbatim account of a murder in the papers. There is a little touch of the criminal in most of us, which demands a little such stimulant now and then it seems. And for those of us who have the right diet from infancy, no subsequent drama can ever intoxicate more satisfactorily than that pair of classics: *The Roly-Poly Pudding* and *The Tale of Mr. Tod*.

Between them, these notable volumes cover a large field of criminal fiction, for they are complementary to one another. Not every stomach is strong enough to bear them both. Those who can enjoy the suave Mr Tod, prototype of all gentlemen criminals, with his taste for family china, and his sandy-coloured whiskers, cannot always endure the coarse obscenity of Tommy Brock, and still more trying to most nerves is that underworld abutting on to Mrs Tabitha Twitchit's comfortable domesticity in *The Roly Poly-Pudding*.

As usual, Beatrix Potter creates her effects with economy. I know of no opening sentences more telling than these, from *Mr. Tod*: 'I have made many books about well-behaved people. Now, for a change, I am going to make a story about two disagreeable people . . ..'

The squeamish had better reopen *Mrs. Tiggy-Winkle* – there is a direct brutality about this introduction reminiscent of Defoe – we are at once in the company of crime. At least we know it for what it is, however. That is less terrifying to me than the opposite technique in *The Roly-Poly Pudding* in which an alien and secretive atmosphere is built up by touches like the little noises in the night that are not very frightening by themselves, but send us under the bedclothes in a cold sweat when they follow close on one another.

At first it is not so much what happens in *The Roly-Poly Pudding* which alarms us, but the way it happens – not so much Tom Kitten's disappearance, for he is a mischievous kitten, but his mother's extreme and somewhat unaccountable agitation at it. Her search continues on a growing note of hysteria – we do not understand it, but we feel our hearts go pit-a-pat in sympathy and so we are already worked upon by the time the real danger is hinted at. And how masterly a hint it is!

> It was an old, old house, full of cupboards and passages. Some of the walls were four feet thick, and there used to be queer noises inside them, as if there might be a little secret staircase. Certainly there were odd little jagged doorways in the wainscot, and things disappeared at night . . .

Not all Dickens' endless description of the 'falling noises' in that most sinister of houses in *Little Dorrit* – a house so evil that it finally perishes of its own internal rot – have more power than this brief revelation.

But still we are not quite sure what we are up against. The mystery thickens: 'somebody' knocks at the front door, 'somebody' else bangs another door and scutters downstairs, there is soot on the kitchen hearth and a roly-poly noise under the attic floor. And even when the truth finally dawns, and the powers of light muster their forces to fight the powers of darkness, we are snatched away from this reassurance to face the terror all over again in the wretched person of Tom Kitten himself.

For while his friends have been searching vainly up and down, Tom, a mere wainscot-width away, has tumbled upon a new world, a world of crime which has existed side by side with his own

familiar existence, in his own house, under his very roof, unsuspected by him. The true ingredients of horror are here. There is nothing so fearful as to discover, foaming, beneath the thin ice of everyday life, the whirlpool of the unknown. In dreams we make this discovery and in dreams it is worst of all, because there we are always alone: Tom's loneliness is the most frightening thing about his adventures. And it would be impossible to emphasize it more cruelly than by the introduction of his only companion (when he was lying bound and helpless):

> . . . a spider, which came out of a crack in the ceiling and examined the knots critically, from a safe distance.
>
> It was a judge of knots because it had a habit of tying up unfortunate blue-bottles. It did not offer to assist him.

Of such are nightmares made.

Compared with this ordeal, the gallant excursion of Benjamin Bunny and Peter Rabbit into Mr Tod's shady domain to rescue their stolen baby bunnies has the companionable air of a crusade. Unlike poor Mrs Tabitha, they also take the initiative from the start, and finally the supreme satisfaction of seeing their enemies attacking one another is theirs. But they have some nasty spots to go through first.

> The sun had set; an owl began to hoot in the wood. There were many unpleasant things lying about, that had much better have been buried . . . It was a shocking place, and very dark.

If the atmosphere in *The Roly-Poly Pudding* belongs to the macabre school of 'mystery and crime' and claims kinship with the House of Usher, *Mr. Tod* is more nearly related to the great adventure stories of the world, from the Odyssey to *The Thirty-nine Steps*, and something of the same heroic spirit animates its characters. Even the villains are not to be despised: there are no lily-livered criminals to be found in Beatrix Potter. And we must not forget that it is the villains whom the story chiefly concerns.

They are a masterly pair. From Tommy Brock's first, stumpy, grinning entrance as he beguiles old Mr Bouncer with his bad jokes

and worse cigars to the final disappearance of them both: 'What dreadful bad language! I think they have fallen down the stone quarry.'

There is not a moment's tedium in their company. The same cannot be said of every notorious villain. If he should be the principal character there is a nice balance to be struck between black and white: our sympathies must not be altogether alienated, for the completely despicable are not amusing, but we must not grow too fond of him either. On the whole Beatrix Potter fulfils these conditions honourably. It is true that I have a sneaking affection for Mr Tod when that fastidious gentleman makes his plans for disposing of Tommy Brock and having so disposed, for cleaning up afterwards:

> 'I will wash the tablecloth and spread it on the grass in the sun to bleach. And the blanket must be hung up in the wind; and the bed must be thoroughly disinfected, and aired with a warming-pan; and warmed with a hot-water bottle.
> 'I will get soft soap, and monkey soap, and all sorts of soap; and soda and scrubbing brushes; and persian powder; and carbolic to remove the smell. I must have a disinfecting. Perhaps I may have to burn sulphur.'

There is a lyrical, almost a Biblical flavour about this intended orgy which appeals to me. But nothing can spoil the dramatic irony of the denouement immediately afterwards:

> He opened the door. . . .
> Tommy Brock was sitting at Mr. Tod's kitchen table, pouring out tea from Mr. Tod's tea-pot into Mr. Tod's tea-cup. He was quite dry himself and grinning; and he threw the cup of scalding tea all over Mr. Tod.

After this, their fate is uncertain. The complacently explicit finales of lesser artists are not for Beatrix Potter. In *The Tale of the Roly-Poly Pudding*, moreover, the criminals get off scot free: not for nothing are Samuel Whiskers, that fat old rat gangster, and his moll, Anna Maria, given the motto 'Resurgam!!!'. For, in spite of their hasty get-away from Mrs Tabitha's, we are expressly told that they flourish ever afterwards, like the green bay tree, and increase beyond belief.

Nevertheless, if crime is not utterly defeated it never triumphs over innocence either. Indeed we are led to believe that criminals daily furnish their own punishment, simply through being the unpleasant people they are. There is no allure about their flourishing. Even the gentlemanly Tod reaps his own deserts as we have seen, not from any detective *ex machina* but through the nemesis of his own wily character.

In our household we keep Beatrix Potter and Shakespeare on the same shelf.

WHAT THE CHILDREN SAID

From numerous accounts of the impact that Beatrix Potter's books have had on children I have chosen just five: an anecdote sent by the author herself to her publisher in 1904; the account of a young American boy's first introduction to the books in the 1920s; the diary of a New Zealand 'children's librarian turned mother' reading with her daughter in the late 1940s; a story from a London primary school in the late 1970s; and a recollection written in 1977 of what a small girl felt when she met 'the bunny lady' early in the 1930s.

To Norman Warne   Dec 29th 04

Dear Mr Warne,

I have been so much amused with this pretty – and rather touching – little anecdote that I am sending it on. Don't trouble to return it; the original copy came to me through friends . . .

With best wishes for the New Year believe me yrs sincerely

Beatrix Potter

A tale of Mary and Eileen aged 5½ and 3½ yrs, who are both very devoted to Peter Rabbit.

I must first explain that these children lost their mother about 6 months ago, and the father thought last Sunday he would take them to the cemetery to see her grave.

Well – he could not quite think how to explain it, so at last he told them that when people died and went to heaven – their friends made a little garden to remember them by, and put up a stone to say whose 'garden' it was. Of course when the children got to the cemetery they wanted to know whose garden each one was – until at last their father had to refuse to read any more. But suddenly they espied one with a rail and little edging round it, and they insisted on being told whose garden it was. It was the 'garden' of a Mr McGregor they were told. Mary and Eileen were perfectly delighted; 'It's Mr McGregor's garden,' they said, 'so he must be dead now, and he can't go after Peter Rabbit any more – that's the hedge Peter Rabbit got through!' and so on!

Their Mother's 'garden' was quite a secondary consideration after this.

And ever since, they tell everyone – 'Do you know Mr McGregor is dead? *We* know it for we saw his "garden", and now he can't run after Peter Rabbit any more!'

I am afraid the tale is badly told, but I did so want Miss Potter to hear it as I thought it was so perfectly charming.

M. Deed

FROM *BEQUEST OF WINGS:*
A FAMILY'S PLEASURE WITH BOOKS
ANNIS DUFF, 1944

I confess that we began to have some doubts of his [Steven's] ever branching off into books about anything other than trains and boats and cars, when he had got well into his fourth year without showing any sign of expanding his interests. Even now we are a bit crestfallen when he makes his usual request at the library for some book that he has already had a dozen times. But you have only to listen to his conversation to know that he begins to have a wide acquaintance with all sorts of books.

The broadening view began to appear last summer. We had taken several of Beatrix Potter's books to the cottage with us, just on the chance that he might begin to reach out for new ideas, and one afternoon, when he came scrambling up the path from the water, 'shedding buttons right and left', I had a sudden vision of Tom Kitten coming up the rockery in like manner. He was ready for a 'little relax', so I took him on my lap and showed him the pictures in *The Tale of Tom Kitten*, very casually at first, and ready to shift to another form of amusement if he showed the slightest impatience. But I need not have been so diffident; he settled down at once, listened to the whole story and looked at the pictures with the greatest interest. A day or two later we read *The Tale of Peter Rabbit* and that was even better. He asked for it every day and began to use words and phrases that pleased him. Picture our delight when we found him one morning, crouched down on the rocks by the water, peering anxiously at one of his little boats that had got washed in under a log, and saying, 'I implore you to exert yourself!'

He has a great liking for the sound and feel of words, partly natural, and partly developed through listening to rhymes and poetry from his earliest babyhood. This, I think, is one reason why he so especially likes Beatrix Potter's books; she uses words so beautifully. He knows half a dozen of her books now, and his conversation is full of piquant phrases: 'That dog won't play with me. I am affronted'; 'I ran very fast, and my heart went lippity-lippity not very fast'; 'There's a fly on the window! Shuh! shuh! little dirty feet!' When he spilled a load of pebbles that he was hauling in his little train, he exclaimed in vexation, 'What is the explanation of these showers of nuts?' . . .

If I should be limited to the books of one author for my children, I think I should certainly choose Beatrix Potter. I wish she could know how much exquisite pleasure she has given us, and how much of our children's delight in their mother-tongue they owe to her.

FROM *BOOKS BEFORE FIVE*
DOROTHY NEAL WHITE, 1954

Three to Three and a Half   *30 December 1948*

This morning was a true midsummer day. Ann and Carol [her daughter] were soon overtired with running about and I suggested stories under the trees. Ann asked for *Peter Rabbit*, which they have been reading about once a fortnight for a long time now. My impression is that they ask different questions every time I read the book and find something new there, much as I find something new every time I pick up *Emma* or *Middlemarch*. The children's classic seems to propagate itself like a bulb, and because of this and because Beatrix Potter's English is so pleasing, I too never become bored with Peter. Yet there are other stories that the children obviously enjoy which reduce me to internal screaming point by the time I've read them ten or twelve times.

Today it was the picture of Flopsy, Mopsy, and Cottontail gathering blackberries which caught their fancy, probably because a few days ago the two of them were over in the section beyond the bush. Together with young Margaret, Carol and Ann enjoyed the illicit pleasures of picking blackcurrants meant for jam. In the story they obviously associated the blackberries with the currants.

Once or twice lately, when I have left the house to go visiting or down to the library or when Dick has left for work in the mornings, Carol has been calling admonishments. I had been a little puzzled because her manner and material have not been a direct imitation of what I or her father would say on like occasions. It has an alien element in it, like an unidentified flavour in a dish for which one thought one knew the recipe. I've just realized that into my normal cautions she had blended Mrs Rabbit's 'you may go into the fields or down the lane, but don't go into Mr McGregor's garden'. Yesterday when I left her next door while I went to town she called back after me, 'Mummy'. Then, holding her head on one side and putting on the half-smiling, half-stern face which signals that she is acting, she said, 'Don't go on the street cars, run over and get some buns, and don't go in Mr McGregor's garden.' . . .

Four to Four and a Half   *15 November 1949*

This afternoon we read *The Tale of Samuel Whiskers or The Roly-Poly Pudding*, another of the birthday Potter books with more intelligence regarding the family of Mrs Tabitha Twitchit, that anxious parent. 'She used to lose her kittens continually, and whenever they were lost they were always in mischief! On baking day she determined to shut them up in a cupboard.'

'Why?' asked Carol. It was not a trivial question. On this and other occasions when she asks 'Why?' I find that she interrupts when the continuity of two events is not apparent. To an adult it may follow: kittens misbehave, therefore they shall be locked up. To Carol it was not a true sequence, hence the query.

The tale of Tom's adventures with the rats and his final humiliation when tied in a roll of dough, represented a more complicated plot than our usual run of stories. Carol itched to get to the pudding incident, so I skipped till we got there and she was thrilled. She seemed to have no sentimental feelings about her hero's predicament at all.

Cousin Ribby in *Samuel Whiskers* with her almost instinctive dislike of the very young is one more notable Potter characterization. 'He's a bad kitten, Cousin Tabitha; he made a cat's cradle of my best bonnet last time I came to tea. Where have you looked for him?' I thought as I read of Carol's devastating verdict on Mrs Z. 'She doesn't want any babies – she doesn't like to get things creased.' . . .

25 November 1949

Even Potters are not ideal with every child on every occasion. In fact I have three Potter failures to record – at least failures with one particular child in one particular environment. *Ginger and Pickles* can be dismissed briefly. The plot hinges on the matter of 'credit' at a village shop, a situation beyond Carol's understanding. The difficulty with *The Tale of Mr. Tod* and *The Tale of Jemima Puddle-Duck* was a matter of geography: the two stories are rural English and Carol is urban New Zealand . . . Here at Littlebourne Road we live on the edge of a reserve of native bushland with never an animal heard or seen, and Carol therefore has no background whatever to enable her to enjoy *Mr. Tod*. Too much had to be explained: why the rabbits couldn't bear the fox, for example. With *Jemima Puddle-Duck* I had to explain about the laying and hatching of eggs, and in both stories the dead weight of information necessary before we could get on with the story killed the pleasure. I skipped hastily to the end of each and put the books away for a year or two.

Four and a Half to Five   *22 June 1950*

Margaret M. has come to stay with us while her mother is in hospital. Both children spent a messy but cheerful afternoon yesterday with dough and rolling pins. Carol made cakes, but Margaret played Martha and concentrated on dumplings. When they asked me to read this afternoon I remembered Tom Kitten's second adventure and brought out *Samuel Whiskers* again. This time Carol was able to understand the story. Now that she is older the book does not make such a long strain on her attention. They listened quite breathless, with only an occasional question. As before, when I read 'On baking day she determined to shut them up in the cupboard' Carol asked 'Why?' They were both puzzled at the size of the farmhouse chimney where Tom Kitten loses his way, and Margaret was quite worried when Tom choked with the smoke. In her short life she has seen her mother go to hospital three times for long periods and the experiences have made her an exceptionally sympathetic child. She asked once or twice whether Tom Kitten was well again. Carol's second 'Why?' occurred when the old rat and his wife fled the Twitchit household after their attack on Tom. 'Why are they going away?' For her it did not follow that flight was the next and logical step.

At this point in the text there is a change from an impersonal narrator into the first person. 'And when I was going to the post . . . I saw Mr. Samuel Whiskers and his wife on the run, with big bundles on a little wheelbarrow . . .' 'You didn't see that,' said Margaret. 'No, but the lady who wrote this book did.'

FROM 'THE AUDIENCE FOR CHILDREN'S BOOKS' ELAINE MOSS, 1979

On one happy morning, a little girl called Sophie brought her pet rabbit to school. He arrived, amid some excitement, with an entourage of thirty stroking, 'ah-ing' five-year-olds in the library at story time. Of course, I had quickly to substitute *The Tale of Peter Rabbit* for whatever I had prepared: a faculty for quick substitution is, I have discovered, one of the linchpins of good teaching. The rabbit was soporific throughout, whether from too many lettuces or too much stimulation, I do not know. But I was grateful. As you may remember, but in all probability do not, right at the beginning

of the story, Mrs Rabbit 'went through the wood to the baker's. She bought a loaf of brown bread and five currant buns.' An insignificant statement you and I might think, one quite overtaken in interest and excitement by Peter's daring adventure and his thrilling escape from the pursuing Mr McGregor. But it was these five currant buns that were the most important element in the story to one listener. That child asked a question which I knew I wasn't supposed to answer. 'Do you know why Mrs Rabbit only bought five currant buns, Miss?'

'You tell me.'

'Because there should've been six, because of Mr Rabbit, but because he had been put in a pie by Mrs McGregor, Mrs Rabbit *decided* [note] to buy only five. One for her, one for Flopsy, one for Mopsy, one for Cottontail, and one for Peter.'

Now, I am not a great believer in the school of thought that presses for stories to be written for this or that therapeutic purpose, though I understand, and sympathize with, the motives behind the pressure. I go along with Ezra Jack Keats on this matter; he once said to me that 'what we must do is reveal people to one another and hope'. There speaks the creative man who realizes that implicit in many stories not specifically tailored for any group need is the very comfort and reassurance looked for by the politically active. *The Tale of Peter Rabbit*, on that morning in my library, was many things besides a good story: nature study, an arithmetic lesson, an occasion for juvenile logic, and an introduction to the rudiments of good housekeeping. You don't go buying a currant bun for a father who is already in a pie. (Beatrix Potter would have liked that.) But has the group that puts pressure on us to provide stories for single-parent families or tales that help children come to terms with death discovered *The Tale of Peter Rab-*

bit, I wonder? I have no doubt that any child with only one parent listening to the story would, if his situation bothered him, have derived comfort from the security of the rabbit-hole 'in a sand-bank, underneath the root of a very big fir-tree'. Children are so much better than we are at sensing connec-tions – and the less we investigate the way they digest and build on what they hear, the better, generally speaking. Which is why it is the children's right to be the audience for a story and to be left in peace to work out for themselves its relevance to their inner lives.

FROM 'SOME WASPS IN THE MARMALADE'
JANE GARDAM, 1977

My mother, discovering *Squirrel Nutkin* in a shop in York when she was on a Mother's Union outing, proceeded to Sawrey, which was not far from our farm. I remember a little, bent, sideways-glancing person looking at me over a gate and a sense of toughness and purposefulness of a high order. I was being led along by a hand – my mother's – and high above me was my mother's face, pink with pleasure at seeing the bunny lady.

She was no bunny lady to me. That she put rabbits in trousers worried me not a bit. They were real rabbits often ridiculous and vicious, and real trousers the sort that ought to be spelt with a W – trowsers. There was ruthlessness in the text as well as the heavenly beauty of the pictures and the sense of immense trouble taken. Look for instance at the drawing of the cat trussed up with string in *The Tale of Samuel Whiskers*, ready to be rolled in pastry. Nobody I think could draw a cat trussed up with string, like breast of lamb with stuffing, without a model. I believe that Beatrix Potter trussed up that cat. She drew it, and its anguished face is a portrait, the portrait of a cat whose relationship with its owner was to say the least a little odd. . . .

I doted and I dote upon Beatrix Potter especially when she is murky – the terrible house of Mr Tod, the awful wet, dark, Lake District afternoon leaden through the windows, the slate, the dripping trees, the fearful smell of decay, the awful teeth of the badger lying on the bed with the dreadful gallows bucket above him. Years later in a lecture to do with Old Norse at the University I awoke to hear the lecturer likening the atmosphere of *Beowulf* to Mr Tod's cottage.

*'An Imaginary Correspondence' was first published in August
1963 in* The Horn Book, *the long-established Boston magazine 'of
books and reading for children and young people'. It was a time when
children's books that crossed the Atlantic (both ways) for publication
were often heavily 'translated', editors believing that children could not
readily accept unusual spelling and terminology. But Rumer Godden
was sparked off to write her imaginary correspondence by another
publishing idea in vogue at the time. 'What really made me angry,'
she writes, 'was the sudden fashionable requirement that children's
books should be written in Basic English, with a vocabulary of 250
words. Even classics were being rewritten in it and young coming
authors made to feel they had to keep within its limitation if they
wanted to be published. One young woman came to me in tears
because they had struck out words in her manuscript, for instance
"forest", but kindly said she could use "trees".'
The page numbers given in the letter of March 7 1963 refer to
the edition of* The Tale of Peter Rabbit *in print at the
time the piece was written.*

AN IMAGINARY CORRESPONDENCE

RUMER GODDEN, 1963

An imaginary correspondence between Mr V. Andal, editor of
the De Base Publishing Company, Inc., and the ghost of Miss
Beatrix Potter, using the word ghost in the old meaning of soul
or spirit. (Some of Beatrix Potter's remarks are taken from her
letters.) She would be shocked to its depth if she knew some of
the things that are going on nowadays in the world of
children's books.

Mr V. Andal to Miss B. Potter   January 18, 1963

Dear Miss Potter:

I am editing for the De Base Publishing Company, Inc., an unusual series of books aimed at beginning readers. The general title is 'Masterpieces for Mini-Minds', and the series will consist of reissues, in a modern production, of famous books that have become classics for children, so that the first reading of the very young will also be an introduction to their own great authors. We are approaching, among others, Hans Andersen, Edward Lear, Lewis Carroll, George MacDonald, Anna Sewell, and Andrew Lang.

The works will be produced whole and entire, though with certain modifications to the text to make them suitable for children of 1963: with this in view we have decided on a limited vocabulary of 450 different words. I have had a list of words prepared by a trio of philologists and I would be glad to send it to you if you are interested. Other words may be added as long as they are within the grasp of a reader from 5 to 8.

Mr Al Loy, our president, has authorized me to pay an advance of $3,000 against royalty upon receipt of an acceptable manuscript along the lines indicated. In addition to the advance there should be continuing payments, for the books will have, besides quality writing, the collaboration of the best illustrators and should enjoy a huge sale.

I hope you will be one of the contributors to this project. If you like to edit your own book, I will be delighted to send you the word list, from which departures can, of course, be made (as long as they come within this age range). If you would rather we edited, this will be undertaken with the utmost care and the De Base Company will be pleased to send you a check for $3,000 as soon as I forward your work.

Cordially,
V. Andal

I send you Hans Andersen's *Ti-ny Thum-my* to see. (Originally issued as *Thumbelina*, and I think now much improved.)

MISS B. POTTER TO MR V. ANDAL   26TH JANUARY, 1963

Dear Mr Andal,

Thank you for your letter. That a request for a fresh issue of my books should reach me after so many years is heartening. The cheque you offer is certainly generous; there are several acres round Sawrey that could with advantage be purchased and given to our National Trust. Publication with another firm would vex my old publishers very much, and I don't like breaking with old friends, but possibly we might arrange to have something published on the American market that would not interfere with my normal sales.

I presume you will want *Peter Rabbit*. I believe my attitude of mind towards my own successful publications has been comical. At one time I almost loathed Peter Rabbit, I was so sick of him. I still cannot understand his perennial success. I myself prefer *The Tailor of Gloucester*, and send you both books to see.

Yours sincerely,
Beatrix Potter

N.B. My books are illustrated by myself.
N.B. I do not understand your second paragraph. How can a work be 'whole and entire' if it is modified? How can a philologist, however gifted, know what words I need? Perhaps I have misunderstood you.

MR V. ANDAL TO MISS POTTER   FEBRUARY 4, 1963

Dear Miss Potter:

I hasten to thank you for *Peter Rabbit*, a most charming tale, and am sure that, when made larger (it must be enlarged – people like to get their money's worth) and given good illustrations, it will make a magnificent book for our series; we shall have our reader's report in a day or two when I shall write to you again. *The Tailor of Gloucester* I have, for the moment, put aside. It has an old-fashioned air about it that might puzzle a child, but perhaps it might be reissued as a 'period piece'. The words would need a great deal of simplification: 'worn to a ravelling' – what could a child make of that?

I am sorry my letter was not clear. The modifications about such words are only those needed to make language more assimilatory to the children of today. In this connection, we believe the advice of our philologists is of value; they are often able to help an author to put his, or her, delightful thoughts into plain words – simple enough for a child to understand.

Yours very sincerely,
V. Andal

MISS POTTER TO MR V. ANDAL   10TH FEBRUARY, 1963

Dear Mr Andal,

Again I do not understand. What do you mean by 'reader's report'? When I sent the manuscript of *Peter Rabbit* to Mr Warne, my original publisher, he read it, made up his mind he liked it, accepted it, and that was settled. Do you really need other people to do this for you? It seems to me a fuss over a very small matter.

I have too much common sense to think that *Peter Rabbit* could ever be magnificent; he is an ordinary small brown rabbit. Nor do I like the idea of the book being enlarged. I have never heard that size was a guarantee of quality, and must point out that my books were made small to fit children's hands, not to impress the grown-ups.

As for the philologists: if an author needs help in putting thought into plain and simple words he, or she, should not try to be an author. It would seem to me you are in danger of using 'simple' in the sense of mentally deficient. Are children nowadays so much less intelligent than their parents?

I have been told I write good prose. I think I write carefully because I enjoy my writing and enjoy taking pains over it. I write to please myself; my usual way is to scribble and cut out and write it again and again. The shorter, the plainer – the better. And I read the Bible (unrevised version and Old Testament) if I feel my style wants chastening.

Yours sincerely,
Beatrix Potter

N.B. My books, as I said, *are* illustrated.

Mr Andal to Miss Potter   February 19, 1963

My dear respected lady:

While disliking having to cross swords with someone as eminent as yourself, I really must enlighten you to the fact that the Old Testament, as reading, is almost totally out of date, not only for children but adults. It has been replaced by the epic screen pictures which, sequestered as you are in your native Cumberland, you may not have seen. These movies are money-spinners, which is heartening as it endorses our belief that there is life in old tales yet – if properly presented. (One of our 'masterpieces' is Genesis, retold in uno- or duo-syllable words.)

Mr Warne could perhaps make his own decision to publish an important manuscript (which is what we want to make *Peter Rabbit* in this new illustrated edition), but that was years ago. Publishing nowadays is such a costly business that we need expert advice. Properly handled, in attractive wrappers, perhaps packaged with one or two others, and well advertised, books for juveniles can become really big business, which is why I hope you will consider carefully our reader's report and let us guide you.

Your well-wisher,
V. Andal

MISS POTTER TO MR ANDAL   22ND FEBRUARY, 1963

Dear Sir,

I am not 'eminent' as you call it but a plain person who believes in saying what she thinks.

Your publishing would not be so costly without all these 'experts' and elaborate notions; indeed, your last letter reads as if you were selling grocery, not books. In my day, philologists kept to what is their real work: to enrich a child's heritage of words – not diminish it.

Yours faithfully,
Beatrix Potter

N.B. The illustrations in my books are integral with the text. They may *not* be separated.

MR ANDAL TO MISS POTTER   MARCH 7, 1963

Dear Miss Potter:

It is with pleasurable anticipation that I send you our detailed reader's report. It has taken a little time to get it – some work was necessary – but, as you will see, apart from some words in the text, some details of plot, new illustrations, fresh names and a larger size for the book, very little has had to be changed.

I very much hope you will co-operate in helping us to bring this classic little book within reach of our children.

Awaiting your favorable reactions,

Again yours cordially,
V. Andal

REPORT AND RECOMMENDATIONS FOR MODERNIZATION OF TEXT AND
ILLUSTRATIONS OF 'PETER RABBIT' BY BEATRIX POTTER

'Mother' must read 'Momma' throughout.

p. 45	'. . . some friendly sparrows . . . flew to him in great excitement, and implored him to exert himself.'	Not all children will be able to identify sparrows; suggest the more general 'bird-ies'; last five words especially difficult; suggest 'to try again' or 'try harder'.
p. 52	'Kertyschoo' for sneezing	Unfamiliar. 'Tishoo' is more usual.
p. 58	'Lippity-lippity'	Not in the dictionary.
p. 69	'Scr-r-ritch'	Might confuse. Onomatopoeia, though allowable, should not distort a word.
Same page	'Scuttered'	Unfamiliar again. Suggest 'ran away and hid', which has the advantage that three out of four words have only three letters.
p. 80	'Camomile tea'	Not in use now. Suggest 'tranquilizer' or 'sedative'.

As well as word limitation, the De Base Publishing Company has decided to use a certain 'thought limitation' so that parents may entrust their children's reading to us with complete confidence. In this connection:

p. 10   We do not think father should have been made into rabbit pie.

Mr McGregor is altogether a too Jehovah-like figure. We want children to *like* people rather than have that out-of-date respect. They must not be left thinking that a little rabbit can be blamed for trespassing and stealing: it was, rather, that he was deprived of lettuce and radishes. Mr McGregor must be made a sympathetic figure.

ILLUSTRATIONS

We now have a report from our art panel, and though these illustrations have charm we believe fresh ones should be used. The rabbits' furniture and clothing are out of date; i.e., the red cloaks used by Flopsy, Mopsy and Cottontail; the length of Mrs Rabbit's skirts; the suspended pan and open cooking fire on p. 8. We therefore propose to commission a young Mexican who specializes in vivid outline drawing. (Less expensive to reproduce.)

NOMENCLATURE

Our bureau reports that while 'Peter' is familiar to most children, Flopsy, Mopsy and Cottontail must be retitled.

Cable from Miss Potter to Mr Andal, 12 March 1963
RETURN PETER RABBIT AT ONCE

Mr Andal to Miss Potter   March 13, 1963

Dear Miss Potter:

We are sorry you have taken this attitude, which I confess seems to us unrealistic and does not take into account public opinion (supported by our own careful poll statistics). We are having much the same reaction from Mr Edward Lear. We saw a charming first version of his poem, 'The Owl and the Pussy-Cat', which then had the lines:

> They sailed away
> For a year and a day
> To the land where the palm tree grows.

and:

> They dined on mince
> and slices of quince
> which they ate with a silver spoon.

lines quite innocuous and satisfactory; but now he has come up with 'bong tree' for the first lines, and 'runcible spoon' for the second, words not only unusual but not even in the dictionary. [The lines are authentic and are in the first draft of 'The Owl and the Pussy-Cat'.]

As he insists on keeping these we have had to return his manuscript as, at your own request, we are returning yours. We can only tell you that it is our opinion, formed by expert advice, that in its present form, parents, teachers, and children will not buy, nor understand, nor like *Peter Rabbit*.

Yours respectfully,
V. Andal

Miss Potter to Mr V. Andal   24th March 1963

Seven million have. I rest in peace.

*'The Aliveness of Peter Rabbit' was delivered as a paper at the
American Association of School Librarians – National Education
Association Book and Author Luncheon in New York in June 1965.
In 1964 Maurice Sendak had been awarded the Caldecott Medal for*
Where the Wild Things Are, *a medal given to 'the most
distinguished American picture book' of the previous year.*

THE ALIVENESS OF PETER RABBIT

MAURICE SENDAK, 1965

NOT LONG AGO I discussed children's books with some colleagues
before an audience of intense and deeply concerned parents. From
the outset, we on the panel made an effort to qualify our position as
experts on children's literature; we all felt the distastefulness of
being dubbed 'experts'. But these parents were full of complaints
about the books being published for their children, and they seemed
to feel that the members of the panel should agree with their
complaints and do something about them.

Their concern, as it turned out, was due in large measure to what
they considered a lack of seriousness and a proper attitude on the
part of the artists and writers now creating books for children.
Some other day I might have a few things to say about that
complaint, but today I want to tell you about another one that was
registered that evening. A gentleman in the audience raised his hand
and with a voice full of righteous fervor declared that no one on the
panel had as yet explained how a book as simple-minded and flat as
Peter Rabbit deserved its prestigious reputation. Worst of all, it
seemed to him to be 'neither fact nor even fancy'. To my horror,
there were some murmurs of approval and even applause. I was
speechless with indignation. How does one respond to such a
sacrilege, except with the natural reply: 'Well, if you can't see!'? But

apparently there are those who can't. What, after all, has *Peter Rabbit* to do with 'the problems confronting our children in today's tangled world'?

It is true that *Peter Rabbit* cannot be used as a handbook for the care and feeding of rabbits, nor can it be easily defined as a fantasy. If poor *Peter Rabbit* doesn't fit into any of these departments, what is all the noise about? At least that is the question the gentleman in the audience seemed to be asking. The answer, of course, is 'Nothing', if one insists on breaking a work of art into bits and pieces for the empty satisfaction of forcing it into some pigeon-hole, a pastime for the unimaginative and the philistine alike.

We working artists on the panel made very plain the pointlessness of assigning this or that book to this or that pigeon-hole. And that just added to the confusion. We agreed among ourselves that, in spite of the differences between the fact book and the fantasy book, *both* should properly come under the heading (if we must have a heading) of imaginative writing. We even agreed that many of the dead objects passing as books today might have been created by misguided artists, the sort who attempt to fit their work into meaningless pigeon-holes under the illusion that factual truth and fictional truth have nothing to do with each other.

It is just here that *I* find confusion. The differences between a tale of fantasy and a factual account are self-evident, but I wonder if those of us concerned with books for the young sufficiently recognize that *any* life-enhancing book is more or less a product of the imagination. I don't mean imagination limited to conjuring up make-believe worlds, but rather an imagination which contributes a sense of life to all worlds, factual and fantastical. To outlaw imagination in any book on the grounds that it is synonymous with fantasy and has nothing to do with a down-to-earth account of, say, the principles of the automobile engine is to distort the meaning of 'imagination' and produce the lifeless.

But I have strayed far from the panel discussion. I think we made it quite clear that there were no oracles seated on the platform that evening. However, for all our efforts, we were treated as experts and not too subtly condemned for being not-too-expert experts. But I don't mind being discredited for failing to care that *Peter Rabbit* is neither fish nor fowl, for being glad, in fact, that this work of the imagination defies pigeon-holing.

That gentleman in the audience contended that the people inhabiting 'the world of children's books' had foisted *Peter Rabbit* onto the public. He, for one, resented that. He saw through the lie; in a word, he saw nothing. What had that silly rabbit to do with the hard facts of life, or even the dream facts? Where was the imagination? Alas, I could not find the words to defend Peter to the gentleman in the audience. How does one defend the obvious? My only impulse was to smash him in the nose. *That* would be defending the honor of Beatrix Potter. Being aware, however, even from the platform, that his height and breadth were greater than my own, I quietly sulked instead. But here, in front of sympathetic and no doubt true-blue Potterites, I can bravely state my case: *Peter Rabbit* transcends all arbitrary categories. It is obviously no more a fact book about the habits of rabbits than it is a purely fantastical tale. It demonstrates that fantasy cannot be completely divorced from what is real; that fantasy heightens and contributes new insights into that reality.

I know that *Peter Rabbit*, for this audience, needs no boosting from me, but I would like to point to a few details that might help make my own feelings about it clear. I will refer, of course, to both words and pictures, for in this book there is no separating them.

Above all, this tiny book vividly communicates a sense of life, and this, I believe, is achieved through an imaginative synthesis of factual and fantastical components. Amazingly, Peter is both endearing little boy and expertly drawn rabbit. In one picture he stands most unrabbitlike, crying pitifully when there seems no way out of his dilemma. In another he bounds, leaving jacket behind, in a delightful rabbit bound, most unboylike, proving what we already know from her published sketchbooks: that Beatrix Potter drew from careful observation of her subject. And how she could draw! – a gift not all illustrators are endowed with.

This book, so apparently simple, smooth, straightforward, is to my eye textured and deepened by the intimate, humorous observations that Beatrix Potter makes in her pictures. Take the birds, for example, that emotionally mirror the action. Flopsy, Mopsy and Cottontail, the good little bunnies, are accompanied by two chipper, pecking birds whose routine busyness seems to represent the humdrum behavior of those cautious three. On the other hand, the bird observing Peter on his dangerous mission has an air of still, sorrowful speculation. He represents, I imagine, the helplessness and concern we feel for Peter. He seems ancient and philosophic in his doomlike observation of Peter's shoe under the cabbage; I can almost see him shake his head. There is nothing chirpy about him. His movements are as quiet as the deadly atmosphere that hangs over Mr McGregor's garden. But there is no mention of birds in the text until much later, when Peter, trapped in the gooseberry net, is implored by three sparrows 'to exert himself'. And what a brilliant threesome! There is such beauty in the drawing, and it is so convincing, that their passionate outcry is almost audible. Peter does exert himself, and escapes in the nick of time from Mr McGregor's dreadful sieve; and the three sparrows, who surely could have flown away long before, have stopped with Peter up to the last moment, and all burst off to freedom together. They are apparently the same three who, near the end of the tale, anxiously watch Peter slip underneath the gate into the safety of the wood outside the garden; three birds who, in Peter's presence, behave almost like guiding spirits. Flopsy, Mopsy and Cottontail attract only garden-variety birds.

I tremendously admire the poetry of Miss Potter's art as she develops this fantastic, realistic, truthful story. There is Peter pathetically slumped against the locked door in the wall; and there is the old mouse, her mouth too full of a large pea to answer Peter's desperate inquiry as to the way to the gate and freedom. She can only shake her head at him, and he can only cry. This tiny scene has the exact quality of nightmare: the sense of being trapped and frightened and finding the rest of the world (in this case, an old mouse) too busy keeping itself alive to help save you.

And last, I recall my favorite scene of the white cat, that lovely creature so prettily painted in the sylvan setting of Mr McGregor's garden. How fortunate her back is turned to Peter, who very wisely thinks 'it best to go away without speaking to her; he had heard

about cats from his cousin, little Benjamin Bunny.' What a typical Beatrix Potter under-statement! For me, this picture marvelously blends opposing images: the sweet surface charm of the delicate watercolor garden domi-nated by an innocent-looking cat who, on closer observation, turns out to be fearful in color; that is, its innocent whiteness becomes a dreadful *absence* of color. The taut, twitching tail and the murderous tension of muscle under the plump, firm exterior betray the untamable cat nature. The poor witless goldfish in the pond at its feet haven't got a chance.

I have tried to suggest the kind of imaginative blend of fact and fantasy, integrated and working together harmoniously, that creates for me the aliveness of *Peter Rabbit*. Fantasy, rooted in the living fact: here, the fact of family, of fun, of danger and fear; of the evanescence of life; and finally, of safety, of mother and love. Altogether the book possesses, on no matter how miniature a scale, an overwhelming sense of life, and isn't that the ultimate value of any work of art? This standard should be applied to every book for the young, and no book can claim the distinction of art without it. *Peter Rabbit*, for all its gentle tininess, loudly proclaims that no story is worth the writing, no picture worth the making, if it is not a work of imagination.

When Marianne Moore, contributed to 'Some of the Authors of 1951 Speaking for Themselves' in the New York Herald Tribune Book Review *on 7 October 1951 she wrote: 'My favorite authors, I think, are Chaucer, Molière and Montaigne. I am attached to Dr Johnson; I also like Xenophon, Hawthorne, Landor and Henry James. I take an interest in trade journals, books for children, and never tire of Beatrix Potter. . . .'*
Tell Me, Tell Me *was first published in* The New Yorker *on 30 April 1960.*

TELL ME, TELL ME

MARIANNE MOORE, 1960

   where might there be a refuge for me
     from egocentricity
and its propensity to bisect,
mis–state, misunderstand
   and obliterate continuity?
     Why, oh why, one ventures to ask, set
flatness on some cindery pinnacle
as if on Lord Nelson's revolving diamond rosette?

It appeared: gem, burnished rarity
    and peak of delicacy –
in contrast with grievance touched off on
any ground – the absorbing
    geometry of a fantasy:
      a James, Miss Potter, Chinese
'passion for the particular,' of a
tired man who yet, at dusk,
      cut a masterpiece of cerise –

    for no tailor-and-cutter jury –
    only a few mice to see,
who 'breathed inconsistency and drank
contradiction,' dazzled
    not by the sun but by 'shadowy
      possibility.' (I'm referring
to Henry James and Beatrix Potter's Tailor.)
I vow, rescued tailor
      of Gloucester, I am going

    to flee; by engineering strategy –
    the viper's traffic-knot – flee
to metaphysical newmown hay,
honeysuckle, or woods fragrance.
    Might one say or imply T.S.V.P. –
      Taisez-vous? 'Please' does not make sense
to a refugee from verbal ferocity; I am
perplexed. Even so, 'deference';
      yes, deference may be my defense.

A *précis*?
   In this told–backward biography
   of how the cat's mice when set free
by the tailor of Gloucester, finished
the Lord Mayor's cerise coat –
   the tailor's tale ended captivity
     in two senses. Besides having told
of a coat which made the tailor's fortune,
it rescued a reader
     from being driven mad by a scold.

Line 8: 'Lord Nelson's revolving diamond rosette' was the chelengk, *a plume of artificial diamonds to wear in his hat, given to him by the Sultan of Turkey after the Battle of the Nile. The Sultan described it as 'a blaze of brilliants, crowned with vibrating plumage and a radiant star in the middle, turning on its centre by means of watch-work which winds up behind'. The* chelengk *was stolen from a museum in London by a thief who believed the diamonds to be real.*

Lines 20-1: 'The literal played in our education as small a part as it perhaps ever played in any and we wholesomely breathed inconsistency and ate and drank contradictions.' Henry James, Autobiography (A Small Boy and Others, Notes of a Son and Brother, The Middle Years), *1958.*

'Beatrix Potter's Places' was first published in December 1967 in Architectural Design *and revised for the April 1988 issue of* Studio International. *As Alison Smithson writes, 'This essay . . . has perhaps proved to be the most memorable to all sorts of architects, who invariably refer to it as "Beatrix Potter's Spaces".* Architectural Design *of the 1950s and 1960s had a very wide foreign audience and, indeed, was the magazine most likely to be seen being carried in Bombay, Singapore, Johannesburg.'*

BEATRIX POTTER'S PLACES

ALISON SMITHSON, 1967

THERE IS A set of small books which are English nursery classics. Their interest for architects is in their detailed and imaginative exposition of a way of life. Architects might, however, be surprised at any suggestion that there is a connection between the houses of Beatrix Potter and those in the postwar styles of Aalto and Le Corbusier: between the house of Mrs Tittlemouse and that for Mr Shodan in Ahmedabad.

Yet the same sort of striving towards good container-spaces in a particular climate and place – even the same sort of forms – can be found in both the books and in the works of a number of inventive architects of the first, second and third generation of the Modern Movement working in the 1950s and 1960s.

A similarity of intention is also evident in the attitudes to objects and possessions. In Beatrix Potter's interiors, objects and utensils in daily use are conveniently located, often on individual hooks or nails, and are usually all the 'decoration' the 'simple' spaces need, or in fact can take. Those things in secondary use, or needing long-term storage, are in special cubicles whose forms define the house space proper – as well as being pleasant spaces in themselves.

Here, then, we find basic necessities raised to a poetic level: the simple life well done. This is, in essence, the precept of the whole Modern Movement in architecture. In their direct handling of the simplest of materials, Beatrix Potter's spaces touch something of the spaces magicked by our architectural masters.

Beatrix Potter's interiors – nearly all cave-like in feeling if not actually so in their moulded surfaces – are designed to meet the need of the individual, and each room is tailored to its function, the group of rooms responding to their context in the environment.

This is not to say that Beatrix Potter was mysteriously in advance of her times: animals were common on greeting cards; boys sold *objets trouvés* such as birds' nests containing eggs taken from the country, which was then still within an early morning's walk of the London slums; the garden character of the Boltons had not been depressed to bird subsistence level by infill development and the mews had not been domesticated. Miss Potter, in her odd way, fitted into what was afoot generally in the arts. What she instinctively felt about spaces – that they should be comforting, responsive and protective – was part of a general realization about spaces common to artists: Whistler's theories and the exhibition gallery walls he coloured; poets who left the cities (for example, Wordsworth choosing the Lake District); architects including the 'small space', the inglenook and minstrels' gallery. In Norman Shaw's Rothbury there was an attempt to break through the classical tradition of ranges of rooms of identical height to provide instead a sequence allowing the particular shape and mood to answer a function serviced by modern means.

It is perhaps interesting to compare the change of imagery in gardening brought about by Gertrude Jekyll to make it typically English as the majority now understand and practise it. Lutyens bicycled over with his fiancée to see Gertrude Jekyll, and his fiancée wrote of the visit: 'the most enchanting person in the loveliest little cottage. Mr Lutyens calls her Bumps . . . After dinner we sat in the chimney corner. A real old chimney with a huge wood fire, and there we sat, and ate almonds and drank hot elderberry wine.' It evokes Peter Rabbit's mother stooping to make camomile tea and the settle in the frontispiece of *Cecily Parsley's Nursery Rhymes*. Architecture, faced with the invention of so many new building types and a massive increase in scale, was already on a gigantic style-trip detour and – perhaps with Ruskin's and Morris's help, both unfortunately without wit – attempting the English 'protoform-fits-function' way out: Norman Shaw de-classifying; Baillie-Scott cottageizing; Unwin canonizing; maybe only Mackintosh managing, before bureaucracy standardizing. In the face of this final degeneration of aims and values, the space of Beatrix Potter might – to the English – appear a dream of childhood, and the Maison Jaoul an old man's New Brutalist sentimentality. But the strivings of the Modern Movement cannot be so easily labelled and brushed off, however far-fetched it might appear to bring nursery books into the fore of its creation. Their inclusion might be totally laughed off as fancy were these books not, in themselves, such 'total manifestations' of the approach of a new spirit, coexistent with a new attitude to the land that would become *'l'espace, verdure, soleil'* of Le Corbusier and so of the Modern Movement in architecture.

Nevertheless, in England, after nearly half a century of aesthetic control, it would be a brave architect who would submit a white house to a County Planning Authority, even though it was suspected that the officers and the lay committee in jurisdiction had read *Jemima Puddle-Duck* and *Mrs. Tiggy-Winkle* more often than a textbook on, say, the effect of motorways on the landscape.

Beatrix Potter, in her concept of town building, was close – in Gloucester under snow and in the 'town' spaces of the fells – to a domestic environment of nowadays *vital* calmness. The dwellings of her people fit the landscape with that sort of anonymity which is only achieved through building in an internally consistent language which is itself an extension of a climate – conscious, aspect/prospect aware, inherited language.

Where others failed in their imagination, Beatrix Potter succeeded in portraying forms entirely suitable for their purpose, which, in their sympathetic inventive reality, are of continuing interest to successive generations.

102

'Tailpiece' was written as a contribution to Volume 12 of
Children's Literature, *published in 1984.*

TAILPIECE: THE TALE OF TWO BAD MICE

SUZANNE RAHN, 1984

THE LAST YEARS of the nineteenth century and first of the twentieth were years of considerable political ferment in England, culminating in the General Election of 1906, which gave the Labour party an unprecedented fifty-three seats in Parliament. 'You'll have a revolt of your slaves if you're not careful,' said E. Nesbit's Queen of Babylon in *The Story of the Amulet*, and she was not alone in her prediction. *The Story of the Amulet* (1906) is very much a product of those days of turmoil, and so, in part and from an opposite political standpoint, is Kenneth Grahame's *Wind in the Willows* (1908), in whose final chapters a lower-class mob of stoats and weasels invades the stately home, Toad Hall, and must be forcibly driven out again. That even a shy, sheltered, comfortably middle-class children's author like Beatrix Potter might be affected by this atmosphere is suggested by her *Tale of Two Bad Mice*, published in 1904.

The story begins with the description of a 'very beautiful doll's-house; it was red brick with white windows, and it had real muslin curtains and a front door and a chimney.' The house is inhabited by two dolls, Lucinda and Jane (the Cook). One day, when Lucinda and

Jane are out for a drive, two mice – Tom Thumb and his wife, Hunca Munca – venture into the doll's-house. They help themselves to the 'lovely dinner' laid out in the dining-room, but when they discover that the food is only painted plaster, 'there was no end to the rage and disappointment of Tom Thumb and Hunca Munca'. They smash the food and 'set to work to do all the mischief they could', especially Tom:

> He took Jane's clothes out of the chest of
> drawers in her bedroom, and he threw them
> out of the top floor window.
>   But Hunca Munca had a frugal mind.
> After pulling half the feathers out of
> Lucinda's bolster, she remembered that she
> herself was in want of a feather bed.

The two mice manage to carry off the bolster, a cradle, some clothes, and several other items before the dolls return to view the scene of destruction. Retribution seems imminent:

> The little girl that the doll's-house belonged to, said, – 'I will
> get a doll dressed like a policeman!'
>   But the nurse said, – 'I will set a mouse-trap!'

But the story ends, rather surprisingly, with the two mice voluntarily paying for the damage they have done; they stuff a crooked sixpence into one of the dolls' stockings on Christmas Eve,

> And very early every morning – before anybody is awake –
> Hunca Munca comes with her dust-pan and her broom to sweep
> the Dollies' house!

Two Bad Mice has always been popular with children. It is a good story; it has suspense and humor and vigorous action and character interest as well, for the bland and ineffectual dolls are a perfect foil for the daring, impulsive, and resourceful mice. It satisfies the young child's strong and complementary needs for adventure and for security, the adventure of disrupting one's world and the security of putting things back just as they were. (It is rather like *Peter Rabbit* in that respect, except that Peter's naughtiness is the outdoor variety – running away, getting lost, trespassing – and the naughtiness of the two mice is the indoor variety, getting into things and playing with them and breaking them.) Finally, as protagonists mice have a particular appeal. . . . Moreover, they are exactly the right size to explore a doll's-house, so that we experience the double enchantment in *Two Bad Mice* of one miniature world superimposed upon another.

But we can also see *The Tale of Two Bad Mice* as something other than a charming nursery story, for like *The Story of the Amulet* and *The Wind in the Willows* it reflects the tensions of its age. The doll's-house itself is a perfect emblem of upper-middle-class smugness and prosperity. Its handsome red brick façade and real muslin curtains conceal not life but a hollow imitation of it. The two dolls, Lucinda who 'never ordered meals' and a Cook who 'never did any cooking', preserve a set of class distinctions that have become meaningless (we see later that they share the same bed). In this world even food no longer nourishes but is valued only for its impressive appearance:

> There were two red lobsters and a ham, a fish, a pudding, and some pears and oranges.
> They would not come off the plates, but they were extremely beautiful.

Taking advantage, like the stoats and weasels of *The Wind in the Willows*, of the absence of the rightful owners, a hungry mob (if we may call two mice a mob) from the lower levels of society invades the doll's-house. When they recognize the false values (symbolized by the inedible plaster ham) of the doll's-house for what they are, they are enraged and set out to destroy them, but they are distracted by the material wealth around them and turn to looting instead. Perhaps they are even a little corrupted by their exposure to luxury, for they steal not only useful things such as the bolster but also a bird-cage and a book-case which (significantly) will not fit into their mouse-hole. The ineffectiveness of the police in dealing with such major civil disorders is shown in the illustration of the 'doll dressed like a policeman'; Hunca Munca is holding up one of her babies to look (perhaps jeer) at him, with no sign of trepidation, while two other mice peer in the doll's-house windows behind his back. The mouse-trap is another matter – something more like martial law – and the illustration of it shows Tom Thumb pointing it out very carefully to his children.

Up to this turn of the story, we might assume Beatrix Potter to be in sympathy with the revolutionary uprising she has depicted; certainly she is in sympathy with the mice rather than with the passive and uninteresting dolls. The ending, however, reveals a political stance unmistakably Conservative. Not only is the property damage paid for, but Hunca Munca becomes a servant to the very dolls she had robbed. The former social order is not only restored but reinforced.

Such a conclusion would go well in harness with what we know of Beatrix Potter's political convictions. According to her biographer Margaret Lane, Beatrix Potter 'by temperament and upbringing was an unshakable Conservative'. Entries in the private journal she kept from 1881 to 1897 show her eager to follow her father's lead in denouncing Gladstone (the Liberal Prime Minister at this time), the supporters of Home Rule for Ireland, and the leaders of the unemployed rioters of 1885. Her day-by-day entries at the time of these riots show clearly that middle-class people like the Potters were frightened not so much by the actual violence of the riots as by the greater violence they might portend. 'Why, they ought to be hung at once like dogs,' she wrote of the four leaders of the riots who stood trial in February 1886. 'I consider they are the most dangerous kind of criminals in existence. A murderer affects but a small circle, they, if unchecked, will cause wholesale slaughter, and ruin society.' Although Beatrix Potter was no longer keeping a journal in 1904, we can see from these entries that the possibility of lower-class uprisings on a large scale was familiar to her in her teens. Her only personal foray into politics was made not too long after *Two Bad Mice*, in the General Election of 1910, when she campaigned vigorously against the Liberal policy of Free Trade [and on the question of tariffs] which had robbed her of her American royalties.

A certain degree of political consciousness, then, was part of Beatrix Potter's outlook and may well have had some influence on her work. Another piece of evidence shows that she did think of her characters in class terms and, specifically, that she mentally categorized her two mouse-protagonists as lower-class, which in the text of the story itself is left somewhat in doubt. She used to amuse her child-friends by sending them miniature letters, supposedly to and from characters in her own books. A surviving letter from Lucinda to Hunca Munca dating from after the events in the story, together with Hunca Munca's reply, makes clear the relative class positions of these two characters. Lucinda refers to herself only in the third person and does not address Hunca Munca directly, while Hunca Munca not only uses the first person but addresses Lucinda with an obsequious 'Honoured Madam':

Mrs Tom Thumb, Mouse Hole
   Miss Lucinda Doll will be obliged if Hunca Munca will come half an hour earlier than usual on Tuesday morning, as Tom Kitten is expected to sweep the kitchen chimney at 6 o'clock. Lucinda wishes Hunca Munca to come not later than 5.45 a.m.

Miss Lucinda Doll, Doll's House
Honoured Madam,
I have received your note for which I thank you kindly, informing me that T. Kitten will arrive to sweep the chimney at 6. I will come punctually at 7. Thanking you for past favours I am, honoured Madam, your obedient humble Servant,

Hunca Munca

Beneath their polished surface, however, these little letters tell a different story. Hunca Munca is *not* coming at 5.45, as requested,  but at 7.00; without wasting time in argument or self-justification, she lets Lucinda know that things will be arranged to suit her convenience, not Lucinda's. Seen from this perspective her 'Honoured Madam' and 'obedi-ent humble Servant' are only the frosting of convention, while 'Thanking you for past favours' may well remind us (and Lucinda) that the dress Hunca Munca wears when she comes to sweep, and even her dust-pan and broom, originally belonged to Lucinda and Jane (Tom Thumb is shown in flight with the broom in one picture). Nomin-ally a servant, Hunca Munca retains not only her self-respect but the upper hand.

In fact, *Two Bad Mice* as a whole does not reflect what we know to have been Beatrix Potter's political opinions with any degree of consistency. If the rampage of the two mice represents a lower-class uprising like the riots that damaged shops and houses in 1885, it is an uprising which we are invited to enjoy and even approve. There is a kind of triumph, as of truth over falsehood, in Tom Thumb's destruction of the plaster ham. There is satisfaction in seeing Hunca Munca, with her 'frugal mind', salvaging what she wants from the doll's-house like Robinson Crusoe and making such good use of it.

And while the mice do pay for what they have stolen or destroyed, they clearly choose freely to do so and are not coerced by the threat of traps or policemen. They make their own terms with the doll's-house world.

Viewing *Two Bad Mice* from a strictly political perspective does not seem to make the best possible sense of it, after all. Another, more personal element was involved in the creation of this story, and we need to understand what part this played before we can resolve the pattern of the whole.

The text of *The Tale of Two Bad Mice* was written near the end of 1903 and the book completed in the summer of 1904. It was Beatrix Potter's fifth book for Frederick Warne and Company, and by now she had grown used to working closely with the youngest of the three Warne brothers, Norman, a sensitive and tactful editor. In spite of the growing disapproval of Beatrix's parents, this fruitful partnership was already ripening from friendship into love, and in the summer of 1905 Beatrix accepted Norman's proposal of marriage – an engagement that ended tragically with his death a few months later from pernicious anemia. *The Tale of Two Bad Mice*, unlike any other of Beatrix Potter's books, deserves to be considered in relation to this biographical background, for it was in large part a collaboration between her and a man she was learning to love. 'It was during the preparation of *The Tale of Two Bad Mice*,' states Leslie Linder, 'that Beatrix Potter and Norman Warne came to know each other well. They cooperated in a way that had not been possible during the writing of earlier books.'

It was Norman who built a mouse-house for the real Tom Thumb and Hunca Munca, Beatrix Potter's pet mice, with a glass front so that Beatrix could observe the mice and sketch them for her illustrations. ('I have had so very much pleasure with that box, I am never tired of watching them run up & down,' wrote Beatrix.) It was Norman who provided Lucinda and Jane. ('Thank you so very much for the queer little dollies, they are just exactly what I wanted . . .') It was Norman who bought the indispensable plaster food. ('I received the parcel from Hamley's this morning; the things will all do beautifully; the ham's appearance is enough to cause indigestion. I am getting almost more treasures than I can squeeze into one small book.') Most important of all, it was Norman who built the doll's-house.

It had been designed for his niece Winifred, and Beatrix had seen and admired it when he was still working on it in his basement workshop; perhaps, indeed, it was at that point that the idea for a story combining his doll's-house and her pet mice first took form in her mind. In February 1904, with the illustrations under way, she planned to use the finished house as a model. Unfortunately, it had already been installed in Winifred's nursery at Surbiton, and Mrs Potter apparently refused to let Beatrix make a visit there; she must have suspected by then that her daughter was enjoying something more than a business relationship with Norman, and she objected strongly to Beatrix's marrying anyone 'in trade'. 'People who only see her casually do not know how disagreeable she can be when she takes dislikes', wrote Beatrix to Norman with unusual bluntness. In the end, Norman photo-graphed the doll's-house inside and out, and the final illustrations were done from his photographs. 'They are very good,' wrote Beatrix, thanking him. 'I do not see why you should be so depressed about the front door! I was going to make mine white & I will alter the top a little.' Her gently teasing, affectionate tone is good evidence of the intimacy steadily growing between them as they worked together on the book.

With this background in mind, it is interesting to conjecture what personal meaning may have been incorporated into *The Tale of Two Bad Mice*. Tom Thumb and Hunca Munca are the earliest and one of the very few married couples among Beatrix Potter's many animal protagonists; is it possible that to Beatrix they represented Norman Warne and herself? If so, the book can be understood as a kind of symbolic projection, not of her present uncomfortable situation but of a future she might have begun to hope for.

The doll's-house, in this interpretation, would stand for the genteel upper-middle-class existence, all surface and no substance, which Beatrix had been born into and stifled by all her life. . . . For Beatrix Potter, as for Ibsen, the doll's-house is a place where stereotyped roles, like those of Lucinda and Jane, disguise the basic fact that dolls have nothing to do. There is even a hint, in one of her letters to Norman, that she consciously identified the doll's-house with a way of life that was uncongenial to her: 'The inside view is amusing – the kind of house where one cannot sit down without upsetting something, I know the sort! I prefer a more severe style.' (She was eventually to prefer a farmhouse.) It would not be surprising if whatever hostility she felt toward her repressive, unloving parents, exacerbated by their frigid disapproval of her friendship with Norman, were expressed symbolically in the violent invasion of a doll's-house as prim as their own home.

The invasion itself consists of three stages – the abortive dinner party, the rampage of destruction, and the looting of the house – each of which represents a successive stage of sophistication. The mice at first assume that the doll's-house food is real food; their rage at having been cheated makes them resolve to destroy everything within reach. But reason prevails; they realize that some things in the house are useful after all and proceed to steal all they can before the dolls return. These stages might show Beatrix Potter herself, progressing from disillusionment (the sociable Warne household was, as Margaret Lane puts it, 'a revelation' to her) to an embittered rejection of everything in her old life, and thence to the more mature realization that she does not really wish to reject *everything*;

there are a few odds and ends worth keeping after all. And if she does rebel and marry Norman without her parents' permission, what could her parents actually say or do to prevent it? The dolls' reaction to the scene of destruction suggests that they would be too dumbfounded to do anything:

> What a sight met the eyes of Jane and Lucinda! Lucinda sat upon the upset kitchen stove and stared; and Jane leant against the kitchen dresser and smiled – but neither of them made any remark.

In the next pages Beatrix goes farther still into this imaginary future, revealing (as is often the case with her) more in pictures than in words. In one place the text says only: 'The book-case and the bird-cage were rescued from under the coal-box – but Hunca Munca has got the cradle, and some of Lucinda's clothes.' The illustration facing it is an exquisite evocation of motherhood. Hunca Munca, wearing one of Lucinda's blue dresses, sits in a chair with a baby in her lap – a baby that is somehow both mouse-baby and human-baby, staring out at us wide-eyed, making a starfish of one hand (paw) and sucking a finger of the other. Beside her, in the cradle, three or four other babies nestle under a pink eiderdown, with their tails dangling out at the foot. These irresistible mouse-children appear in the three following pictures as well. In one Hunca Munca shows them the 'useful pots and pans' from the doll's-house, on the next page she holds up the smallest to squeak at the

policeman, and in the third she and her husband instruct their children about the mouse-trap, Hunca Munca still holding the smallest baby in her arms. In all these pictures Hunca Munca is dressed, as if to acknowledge the dignity of her new role. The children are so important in these pictures that we might wonder at their not being mentioned in the text. But the text, of course, was finished before Beatrix Potter even began work on the pictures. It seems that as the book developed, and as it became more of a collaboration with Norman Warne, it also became more and more a hopeful imagining of what their lifelong collaboration might be.

The final pages make sound emotional sense after this. As a Victorian daughter – and, although she did eventually win a life of her own, she remained a dutiful daughter to the end of her days – Beatrix would always have felt a little guilty at having defied her parents' wishes. So, as Hunca Munca, she returns regularly to the doll's-house and makes symbolic reparation for the disruption she has caused there. The final mood is one of reconciliation between mouse-hole and doll's-house.

Which interpretation of *The Tale of Two Bad Mice* is the better one – the political or the biographical? A complete appreciation of the book must, I think, include both. Drawing upon her vivid memories of the riots of 1885, Beatrix Potter recreated in symbolic form the class conflict of her time, expressing what the middle classes feared and the outcome they hoped for – peaceful preservation of the social structure. And yet, her personal circumstances in 1903 had subtly altered her point of view; she herself had been made to feel oppressed and impatient with those in power over her. And so Tom Thumb and Hunca Munca are not punished but keep the loot and make their own terms of payment. At the same time, working on this book with a man she was beginning to love and thwarted in this relationship by her parents' small-minded disapproval, Beatrix Potter created a story which expresses both her inner rebellion against them and their stultifying way of life and her hope for a fulfilled and happy future. All this – and more, of course – is interwoven in *The Tale of Two Bad Mice*.

For many years Paul Jennings had his own column in The Observer, *one of London's oldest Sunday newspapers, under the by-line 'Oddly Enough'. His piece about the Potter translations was published on 31 May 1953.*

ODDLY ENOUGH: ON BEATRIX POTTER TRANSLATED

PAUL JENNINGS, 1953

IT IS DIFFICULT to decide whether translators are heroes or fools. They are surely aware that the Afrikaans for 'Hamlet, I am thy father's ghost' sounds something like '*Omlet, ek is de papap spook*', and that an intense French actor, beginning Hamlet's speech to Gertrude with '*Mère, mère,*' sounds exactly like a sheep. In Denmark the film *King Kong* had to be called *Kong King* because '*Kong*' means 'King' in Danish. Seeing a book in shops all over France with the title *Ainsi en emporte le vent*, like a line from Lamartine, I took a long time to realize it was *Gone with the Wind*.

The racial realities of language have become mere intellectual concepts to the translator. He floats over the world in a godlike balloon. The babble of voices under the arches of teeming cities, the infinite variations of uvula and hard palate, the words formed in tribal battles and in tales over the winter hearth, float up to him in a vague, jumbled unity, rich but disembodied, like a distant cooking smell.

Paradoxically, the more a work expresses some special national genius, the more it attracts translators. Until recently I had thought the supreme example of this was *Jabberwocky* done into French, German, and even Latin ('*ensis vorpalis persnicuit persnacuitque*'). But now I perceive that something even more secret and English has attracted them; the children's books of Beatrix Potter.

Quite apart from their literary style, these have the same 'central' symbolic appeal as Jane Austen. Jemima Puddle-Duck, Mrs Tiggy-Winkle, Ribby, Duchess and the rest of them live in a transcendentalized English village, where shops with bottle-glass windows doze in an endless summer afternoon, and nothing changes. No one has heard of foreigners, just as the Napoleonic Wars are never mentioned in Jane Austen.

The moment even the titles are translated we are very much aware indeed of foreigners, of Europe. Here are some:

FRENCH

Sophie Canétang (Jemima Puddle-Duck)
Noisy-Noisette (Squirrel Nutkin)
La Famille Flopsaut (Flopsy Bunnies)
Jérémie Pêche-à-la-Ligne (Jeremy Fisher)

DUTCH

Tom Het Poesje (Tom Kitten)
Jeremias de Hengelaar (Jeremy Fisher)

WELSH

Hanes Dili Minllyn (Jemima Puddle-Duck)
Hanes Meistres Tigi-Dwt (Mrs. Tiggy-Winkle)

ITALIAN

Il Coniglio Pierino (Peter Rabbit)

SWEDISH

Sagan om Pelle Kanin (Peter Rabbit)

GERMAN

Die Geschichte von Frau Tigge-Winkel
Die Geschichte Der Hasenfamilie Plumps (Flopsy Bunnies)

Who *are* these characters, we ask? Well may the inhabitants of the Potter village peep from behind their dimity curtains as this babbling procession pours down the quiet street. Here comes Sophie Canétang, a Stendhal heroine, acutely analysing love with a cavalry officer and a *petit bourgeois* – but respectable compared with the awful Mauriac Famille Flopsaut, festering with hate, ruining the brilliant son who will never get to Paris; compared with the gaudy career of Noisy-Noisette, the Mata Hari of the twenties, as depicted by Colette, or the Maupassant Pêche-à-la-Ligne, the quiet angler who pushes his mistress's husband into the trout pool.

Behind these comes Tom Het Poesje, a king of Dutch Till Eulenspiegel, half jester, half highwayman, a doubtful figure in leather jerkin, plaguing the burghers with rather unfunny practical jokes. Then there is a momentary silence as Jeremias de Hengelaar, the fourteenth-century mystic, shuffles by, pondering on the One.

What on earth does Dili Minllyn, thinking of the April clouds sweeping over her white farmhouse on the green Welsh hill, of the clock ticking on the silent dresser, have to say to Il Coniglio Pierino, the swarthy Sicilian bandit, or to the Nordic hero Pelle Kanin, seen through smoke and fire, howling songs against the northern wind on long-prowed ships?

And who, in this village, is going to be interested in the story of Frau Tigge-Winkel, the widow of a Prussian general who revolutionized something or other in 1874? To say nothing of the Hasenfamilie Plumps I.G., a lesser version of the Krupp dynasty, an endless succession of stern characters extending the family factories in the Ruhr . . .

Almost it is unfortunate that the children in the village, who have one language and one vision, will not see them.

Since the first publication of 'On Beatrix Potter Translated' some of the above books have changed their publisher and new translations have been made. Noisy-Noisette *has become* Noisette l'écureuil, Tom Het Poesje *is now* Poekie Poes, Il Coniglio Pierino *is* La Storia di Peter Coniglio, Frau Tigge-Winkel *is* Frau Igelischen, *and* Der Hasenfamilie Plumps *are* Den Flopsi Kaninchen.

Nicholas Tucker was invited to give the Sixth Linder Memorial Lecture to the Beatrix Potter Society on 15 May 1986. The lectures are given every year to commemorate the contribution to Potter studies made by Leslie Linder and his sister, Enid, in the 1950s and 1960s, and speakers are asked to consider the work of Beatrix Potter in the light of their own specialist knowledge. This slightly shortened version of Nicholas Tucker's talk was published in full by the Beatrix Potter Society in 1989 with the title 'Peter Rabbit and the Child Psychologist'.

SOME FURTHER ADVENTURES: PETER RABBIT AND THE CHILD PSYCHOLOGIST

❦

NICHOLAS TUCKER, 1986

. . . ONE MEASURE OF Beatrix Potter's remarkable success is the way that through her own powers of creative intuition she was able to write best-sellers for children without dreaming of undertaking any sort of prior research. Far from being purely child-centred, her writings for children always share a fine balance between presenting things from a child-like point of view while at the same time periodically confronting a young audience with essentially adult examples of language and understanding. In this way young readers are both at home in her books and also conscious of travelling towards new experiences. Approaching her stories is therefore like meeting an old friend also capable from time to time of mounting the odd shock or surprise. No wonder small children often look so intent when hearing her stories, sometimes no matter how often before. Within nearly all of them readers are required to advance at some moments into the unknown while at others they can feel thoroughly at home in comfortable and familiar surroundings. This pattern of advance and retreat can be found over a whole range of ideas and emotions in Beatrix Potter's books, and also in her use of language.

As it is, her stories are usually told in only a few words per page, making it possible for young readers sometimes to learn them by heart. Keeping to a minimum of text can be more popular with children than with adults, given that many parents often want as much on the page as possible in order to get what looks like their full money's worth. But keeping language spare and surrounding pictures with plenty of white space greatly helps inexperienced eyes in the task of isolating essential detail from mere background information. Short sentences, simple vocabulary and basic plots also help with early understanding. Yet having won her young reader's confidence in this way Beatrix Potter is never above dropping in the odd surprise as well. Take perhaps her most famous sentence, now further immortalized in *The Oxford Dictionary of Modern Quotations*.

It is said that the effect of eating too much lettuce is 'soporific'.

I have never felt sleepy after eating lettuces; but then *I* am not a rabbit.

No ordinary child will recognize the word 'soporific', but this will not matter since its meaning is explained quite clearly in the next sentence. But it is not included here as part of a self-conscious attempt to increase a child's immediate vocabulary – something Enid Blyton occasionally tried to do so painfully in her stories, with sentences like: 'An ambulance – you know, the van that ill people are taken to hospital in.' Rather, Beatrix Potter included it because it sounded right, just as she wanted *The Tale of Benjamin Bunny* to end with the phrase 'rabbit-tobacco', explaining to her publisher that, 'It is rather a fine word'. As a student herself of ancient nursery rhymes in the British Museum Library, she was long familiar with examples of language in children's literature where sound sometimes triumphantly takes over from sense (as for example in the rhyme *Pop goes the weasel!*, which still eludes convincing explanation today as to its real meaning, despite modern scholars' best efforts). Later on in life Beatrix Potter was to keep by her bedside not only a Sheep Breeders' Manual but also a copy of the King James Bible, for more daily acquaintance with language which again often combines the simple with the memorably archaic or exotic. But while Beatrix Potter mostly eschewed truly obscure uses of language in her books, she often wrote in the measured indirect speech of one adult addressing another. Phrases such as 'dignity and repose' or 'vindictive and sandy-whiskered' while very possibly foreign to many in her young audience also possess a curiously attractive rhythmic remoteness. Years later another brilliant author for children, Joan Aiken, recalled phrases like 'cynical immorality' or 'blatant indecency' she had come across in Kipling's story *Stalky & Co.* Although too young at the time to have any idea what they meant, their combination of musicality and novelty made them immediately interesting to her, to be repeated endlessly to herself during odd moments of the day. I imagine other children have sometimes done the same thing with some of Beatrix Potter's more stately phrases as well.

This is not to say that all her language shared the same qualities of quaint formality. At other moments she could fight hard for words not currently in respectable use. At one time her publishers objected to 'scuttered' in an evocative sentence from *The Tale of Samuel Whiskers:* 'Once they heard a door bang and somebody scuttered downstairs'. Beatrix Potter conceded that she could not find the word in her dictionary, but if this meant she was not allowed to use it, could she substitute 'scurried' instead? Fortunately her publishers relented over 'scuttered', easily the best word to describe the furtive movements of rats' paws moving along at top speed. Elsewhere she ended *The Tale of Little Pig Robinson* with the sentence: 'He grew fatter and fatter and more fatterer. . . .' A strange last word to set alongside some of her other rather formal vocabulary, but typical in its daring of the range she offered young readers, stretching from examples of early infantile errors right through to extracts from sophisticated drawing-room conversation. This is true variety, compared with much of the monotonously simplified prose on offer to the young today, where modern children's encyclopedias sometimes boast the services of special 'Readability Consultants' to make sure that vocabulary always remains easy enough. Rewritten versions of Beatrix Potter's own stories have appeared recently with the same end in mind. But I doubt whether they are as popular as the originals, either with children or with those adults required to read them aloud as many times as the occasion demands.

Her actual story-forms can also at times be equally demanding. Books like *The Story of A Fierce Bad Rabbit* are very simple while others, such as *The Tale of Little Pig Robinson*, are altogether more complex. Titles in the middle of this range also pose young readers with odd problems every now and again. Despite the fact that infants sometimes become confused by the existence of sub-plots, Beatrix Potter provides several examples of parallel action in her books. In *The Tale of Jemima Puddle-Duck*, the collie dog Kep leaves

the main action for a moment in order to enlist the help of two fox-hound puppies against the smooth-talking, foxy-whiskered gentleman. Later on they all converge on him and Jemima just in time. An infant familiar with this story will eventually come to expect this arrival even though both the dogs and any evidence of their plotting have been absent for several pages. Learning in this way to merge what is in front of your eyes with what you already know but cannot see at that moment is one of the great intellectual tasks facing all infants.

Stories that simply follow one main character through from start to finish cater for only the first stages of this type of skill. Beatrix Potter often offers something more ambitious. In *The Tale of Samuel Whiskers* the kitten Moppet spies the old woman rat in the kitchen; thirty pages later the same scene is enacted again, this time from the point of view of the rat. Children used to the idea that story events always flow in an inevitable serial order of time will have to do some rethinking here, just as they will when mention is made of a 'roly-poly' noise; something only fully explained more than thirty pages later when Maria and Samuel are at last seen trying to make their elusive pudding. Adult readers well used to stories playing tricks with time over a series of parallel actions will of course have no trouble here, but for very young readers the intellectual effort required to hold all such events together can be quite considerable. But with a story also as exciting as this, the incentive towards full understanding will be particularly strong and as such potentially very effective.

As an illustrator, Beatrix Potter's unique mixture of simplicity and complexity is also on offer to young readers. Her animal characters are made extra approachable through the skilful way in which she cuts down on external detail such as the quantity of a rabbit's whiskers or of a pig's bristles. Like Walt Disney later on, she realized that young eyes find it easier to cope with drawings depicting only a few main features of the object described: thus the simplified typewriters or bicycles of a Disney film, together with Mickey Mouse's three-fingered, gloved hand. In *The Tale of Mrs.*

Tiggy-Winkle, our first view of this excellent clear-starcher is of someone almost enveloped in print gown, large apron and striped petticoat. Dressing animal characters in human clothes makes them easier for infants to first identify who they are and then to accept them as rounded characters in their own right. By contrast, the real hedgehog Beatrix Potter paints on the last picture of the book is now indeed true to life, but as the author points out herself:

> . . . *how* small she had grown – and *how* brown – and covered with PRICKLES!
> Why! Mrs. Tiggy-winkle was nothing but a HEDGEHOG.

And as such, no longer a character capable of appealing to the very young with anything like the same power as the humanized animal previously encountered.

Beatrix Potter's other pictures often tend to concentrate on the salient details of each scene in a way especially suited to infants unused to looking at illustrations and needing help in learning how to pick out the most relevant detail. Sometimes her pictures only take up half a full page, with surrounding white space substituted for the mere amassing of more potentially confusing detail. But having got young eyes to focus on main rather than extraneous objects, she is again good at getting these same eyes to work extra hard to extra effect. In *The Tale of Peter Rabbit* the existence of our hero in one picture can only be inferred by the tips of his ears sticking out from a watering-can (a detail also used for the kitten Moppet in *The Tale of Samuel Whiskers*). As it is, infants often find visual clues like this rather difficult when it comes to having to work out the whole from the part. While older readers can straightaway imagine the rest of

the rabbit in the watering-can, infants usually find it easier to see things for what they are only when they are clearly visible in their totality. Like first-time viewers in the early days of the cinema who during close-ups would sometimes wonder what had happened to the rest of the actor's body, infants too can sometimes have their own problems with incomplete pictures. So illustrations showing only Peter's ears or Mr McGregor's descending boot can issue something of a challenge. Yet so great is the interest in *The Tale of Peter Rabbit* at these particular life or death moments that even the youngest children will want to make the extra effort needed to decipher what is really going on as soon as they possibly can.

Her pictures also sometimes take a story on in advance of their written text. In *The Tale of Mr. Jeremy Fisher* an enormous trout swims up under his frail lily-leaf boat. Children know what is about to happen well before he does himself. Being wiser than those in the story and sometimes a little ahead of those  reading it out aloud can be deeply satisfying to infants usually only too well aware of how little they can predict happenings in the adult world around them. In her prose too, Beatrix Potter also provides young readers with further nods and winks of this kind. They but not poor stupid Jemima Puddle-Duck will soon understand exactly why the 'bushy long-tailed gentleman' so specifically required sage, thyme, mint, two onions and parsley for the special dinner party he was so intent upon. They but not Little Pig Robinson will quickly realize why the ship's cook never tires of boiling up porridge specially for him. Learning that an apparently benign action can sometimes act as a disguise for something less pleasant is another of the necessary tasks of childhood, and a particularly difficult one. This is why sarcasm always puts infants in a quandary, when honeyed words still manage to imply a different meaning from their surface message. Once again, Beatrix Potter is on hand to offer some clues about this type of mystery, made that bit easier here by appearing in the context of a picture story that can be read over and over again until it is fully understood.

But whatever the level of stimulation in print or pictures, children – like the rest of us – will seldom be tempted to make any excessive demands upon their intelligence unless there are strong inducements so to do. Where reading is concerned, the best motivator is still a good story, and in Beatrix Potter's case some of her most successful tales follow traditional plots featuring the predator and the preyed upon already familiar from fairy stories the world over. These can be a little frightening at times, but she always balanced such stories with others where much less happens and there is instead, as in *The Tale of Mrs. Tiggy-Winkle*, a greater emphasis on purely domestic detail. Children who possess a number of her books can therefore pass from descriptions of brushes with near death to accounts of very mild mischief. Such variety in one author is another clue to her popularity, where children consulting the end-pages featuring all her characters can recreate in their own minds everything from Tom Kitten's near disastrous adventures through to the much milder stories of Squirrel Nutkin or Mrs Tittlemouse.

Even so, it is still true that the majority of Beatrix Potter's stories flirt with the idea of danger, and this has sometimes been used as grounds for complaint. Such criticism had more force during the times when children's early literature was often seen as no more than an excuse for a sentimental excursion into what the French writer Marcel Aymé once described as 'stupidity, lies and hypocrisy'. Today we no longer believe quite so fervently in protecting young children from all intimations of cruelty or danger in literature. For one thing, television is already telling them a quite different story; for another, we no longer find it impossible to admit that the seeds of adult aggression may also lie in even the smallest child, however angelic in looks or external behaviour. The modern psychologist would therefore advise parents not to distance their children too much either from the possibilities of danger from outside (saying 'No!' to strangers), or else from knowledge of their own occasional capacity for violence in thought or deed. Peddling false notions of security to the young, by contrast, while initially comforting may simply postpone the day when certain hard truths have to be faced both about themselves and the world around them.

Beatrix Potter once put down her initial success to: 'The accidental circumstance of having spent a good deal of my childhood in the Highlands of Scotland, with a Highland nurse girl, and a firm belief in . . . the creed of the terrible John Calvin.' Clearly there was little room for false optimism about the world here. From childhood she also knew how to boil down and skin various small animals and was as familiar with the natural cycle of eater and the eaten as any other child brought up at a time when the workings of the food chain were more visible than they are today, including the part played in it by farmers and butchers. Like her great-grandfather Abraham Crompton, who used to eat snails alive picked from the ivy-covered walls of his garden, she had little time for false sentiment towards animals, fond though she was of them in individual cases. In the world first of a gifted naturalist then later of a successful sheep farmer, animals must always know their place, even when this may turn out to be on the dining-room table surrounded by vegetables and gravy.

This type of tough-mindedness is evident throughout her stories, sometimes as a mild form of gallows humour. As Aunt Dorcas observes so feelingly in *The Tale of Little Pig Robinson*, 'what possible pleasure can there be in entering a shop where you knock your head against a ham? A ham that may have belonged to a dear second cousin?' Elsewhere Little Pig Robinson is described as 'A pork pie walking on its hind legs', and soon has to learn such facts of a pig's life for himself and almost too late. Not for him the charmed life led by pig characters in certain other children's books

since, where pigs are first allowed to get as fat as possible then stay that way until an honourable old age. In Beaxtrix Potter's stories, pigs like most other animals must always watch out for predators, even when these happen to be human.

But while this type of realism can be found in some of her stories, Beatrix Potter still on the whole believed in tempering the wind to the shorn lamb where the harshest facts of country life are concerned. While other subsidiary animal characters sometimes disappear, Tom Kitten, Jeremy Fisher and all her other main characters are allowed to survive through to a happy ending. In her illustrations meanwhile, the sun shines constantly and flowers are forever in bloom – the very picture of rural serenity. Even Mr Tod's famous house, 'something between a cave, a prison, and a tumbledown pig-stye', does not really look so bad against a background of lakeland mountains bathed in a setting sun. So when her prose sometimes turns a little dark, the illustrations continue to reassure, presenting a picture of the Lake District both gentle and golden. If occasionally she went over the top, such as including an illustration of the pie in which Peter Rabbit's father ended his life, she was not averse to changing her mind later on, in this case dropping the picture altogether from the fifth and all subsequent printings.

Children themselves often bring a contradictory mixture of needs and emotions to their favourite reading matter. While they don't want to be badly frightened, they also don't wish to be bored. While they are curious about the real world they also like sharing moments of fantasy where everything follows childish rather than adult rules. While they don't want to be hectored in print they still like stories containing among other things reasonably strong and easy to understand morals. While they enjoy some examples of adult language, they also like stories told in the main in strong, simple English, neither over-sentimental nor unnecessarily stark and abrupt.

On all these scores, Beatrix Potter in the main got the balance almost perfectly right. She has happy endings, but also teaches that punishment can follow carelessness and greed, and that the weak should always be wary of the strong – a lesson that will not be lost on infants already familiar with the ways of older siblings or some bigger children at the nursery class or playgroup. She shows animals in their natural habitat at one moment, then dressed up like little humans at another. The things they do also contain a mixture of the human and animal, from everyday childish things such as playing, eating or disobeying mother down to truly primitive behaviour such as shameless stealing, invading another's territory or plotting another's death. Her language is an adroit mixture of the adult and the child, with formal Edwardian English suddenly giving way to expressive infantile phrases like 'lippity-lippity' or 'scr-r-ritch, scratch, scratch, scritch'. Only in *The Tailor of Gloucester* does she let her penchant for unfamiliar, fine-sounding words take over to an unwise extent, both for children themselves and for those adults struggling to explain or even pronounce words like 'paduasoy', 'chenile' or 'tambour stitch'. . . . But in general she was also way ahead in her understanding that language, pictures and imaginative situations in books are often most interesting when they offer from time to time examples of both an adult and a child's perspective on things. Strictly child-centred language in stories, by contrast, can sometimes tell us as much about an author's limited vision of childhood as it can about children's actual capabilities.

Beatrix Potter achieved such understanding through her gifts as a children's writer and illustrator. Reading her when young is voyage both of recognition and of discovery. Reading her now as a developmental psychologist is to realize that success in communicating with children is not always best managed by following theories or conducting research. Instead, Beatrix Potter's works are a testament to the value of intuition married to writing and artistic skills, themselves the product of a long apprenticeship in getting things right in the way known only to creative genius.

PETER RABBIT IN *THE TIMES*

On 10 August 1990 an item in The Times *Diary reported that work would start shortly in London on a £12 million film,* The Adventures of Peter Rabbit, *'starring Peter, Mrs Tiggy-winkle the hedgehog and the rest of the furry and prickly ensemble created by Beatrix Potter'. The film would be made by Hilltop Films, the team responsible for 'the hugely popular* Snowman'. *The report continued, 'Producer John Coates insists the celluloid Peter will remain faithful to the Potter original. "We don't have to worry about taking anything out. Peter is morally and ethically clean," Coates assures us . . . Director Dian[n]e Jackson also intends to avoid a grim ending. The film will close as Peter's best friend Benjamin Bunny walks down the aisle with his new wife Flopsy Bunny.'*

Four days later the first letter appeared in The Times.

Bad bunnies

FROM MR CHRISTOPHER PRESTON   AUGUST 14 1990

Sir, I am astonished at the extraordinary assertion in today's Diary (August 10) from Mr John Coates, producer of the forth-coming Beatrix Potter film, that *Peter Rabbit* is 'morally and ethically clean'.

We are told unequivocally that Peter 'was very naughty'. He deliberately disobeyed his mother as soon as her back was turned, and he and his cousin Benjamin were evidently habitual petty thieves.

As for spanking, which we are told is being banned from Noddy books, Peter and Benjamin are not merely spanked, but whipped with a switch by old Mr Benjamin Bunny, who is guilty not only of child abuse but of naked and unprovoked aggression against a harmless cat.

Incidentally, Benjamin and Flopsy, who are to be married in the film, are first cousins; but perhaps this does not matter with rabbits.

Yours faithfully,
Christopher Preston

Bad bunnies

FROM MR MICHAEL JONES   AUGUST 22 1990

Sir, Master Peter Rabbit is protected by our criminal law from having his reputation sullied by the indiscretions of his youth. Although apparently guilty of two offences namely criminal damage and theft (of Mr McGregor's lettuces, radishes and French beans) I am sure that Mr Christopher Preston (August 14) would agree that Peter is under the age of criminal responsibility.

Justice would be served by Mr McGregor seeking compensation against Mrs Rabbit in the county court under the small claims procedure.

Yours faithfully,
M. Lewis Jones

Bunnies at law

FROM MR A. D. PARR   AUGUST 23 1990

Sir, Messrs Preston and Lewis Jones (August 14 and 22) appear to be treading on dangerous ground in their appraisal of the activities of Peter Rabbit.

One must bear in mind that the evidence against Peter is purely circumstantial and almost entirely based upon the scurrilous accusations of one Beatrix Potter. Ms Potter's writings have made similar accusations on more than one occasion (e.g.

one Squirrel Nutkin and various mice with urban deprivation problems).

I suggest that it may pay Peter Rabbit to consult lawyers. A claim for damages for libel should put an end to these unsubstantiated rumours.

Yours faithfully,
A. D. Parr

Bunnies at law

FROM MISS JANE THURSTON-HOSKINS   AUGUST 24 1990

Sir, It is Mrs Rabbit who should pursue a claim against Mr McGregor for the murder and subsequent consumption of her husband (letters, August 14, 22, 23).

Peter's behaviour is simply a reaction to this terrible trauma and he should be referred to a suitable counsellor.

Yours faithfully,
Jane Thurston-Hoskins

Bunnies at law

FROM MR JOHN HARVEY   AUGUST 28 1990

Sir, Your correspondent, Master Lewis Jones (for it is he, August 22), refers to Peter Rabbit being under the age of criminal responsibility and thus not subject to the full rigours of the law for his so-called 'crimes' against Mr McGregor and his garden. Poohsticks!

In fact, P.R. was a freedom fighter engaged in rural terrorism against a system which supported a bloated, land-owning capitalist. Old McGregor wanted very much to *fricasser* our hero, and would surely have done so on several occasions had there not been staunch chums on hand imploring Peter to exert himself in escape attempts. So much for justice!

Yours etc.,
John Harvey

Bunnies at law

FROM HIS HONOUR JUDGE P. J. FOX, QC   AUGUST 29 1990

Sir, Mr McGregor should beware Mr Jones's advice (August 22) to sue Mrs Rabbit in the county court lest she counter-claim under the Fatal Accidents Act in respect of her bereavement and loss of her husband's support which would far outweigh the value of the plaintiff's vegetables.

Whether or not Mr Rabbit was the author of his own misfortune might then be the principal issue, Beatrix Potter giving evidence only that he 'had an accident' and 'was put in a pie by Mrs McGregor'. It would be hard-hearted to find against the widow.

Yours faithfully,

Peter Fox

THE TIMES (Third Leader)   September 1 1990

CRIMES OF PETER RABBIT

As the Middle East totters on the brink of war and governments strive to fend off economic recession, an encouraging glimmer of light shines through the darkness: *Times* readers have rediscovered Peter Rabbit.

An item in *The Times* Diary three weeks ago reported that while Noddy was being taken to the cleaners – golliwogs and spanking sessions have been censored – Beatrix Potter's most celebrated hero was to star in a £12 million film. The producer assured his public unequivocally that Peter was morally and ethically squeaky clean.

But was that so? His biographer described him as 'very naughty'. Readers have pointed out that he not only disobeyed his mother but along with his young cousin, Benjamin Bunny, was a habitual thief and mischief-maker – despite the whippings dealt out by Bunny Senior.

Correspondents who have leapt to his defence have argued that Peter was below the age of criminal responsibility. Though guilty, it would seem, of two offences, namely criminal damage and theft (of Mr McGregor's lettuces, radishes and French beans), his youth should have saved him from the full majesty of the law. Justice would best be served, suggested one reader, by Mr McGregor seeking compensation against Peter's mother under the small claims procedure in the county court.

On the other hand the aggrieved Mr McGregor should beware of pressing his case against widow Rabbit, who could file a counter-claim against him in respect of the loss of her late husband's support. How far Mr Rabbit was the author of his misfortune would probably be the principal legal issue if the case were heard under the Fatal Accidents Act. But the evidence that he was 'put in a pie by Mrs McGregor' would probably sway the court against the plaintiff – and in favour of the widow. The consequent damages payable by the gardener would far exceed the cost of his own vegetables.

Peter Rabbit was not alone in setting a poor example to our children. Squirrel Nutkin and Tom Kitten were young tearaways and Samuel Whiskers a bit of an old rogue. Jemima Puddle-Duck was more sinned against than sinning. She was always such a bad sitter that her eggs had to be taken away at birth and placed in care. But perhaps poor Jemima was a frustrated careerist for whom the farmer should have provided a crèche.

Winnie the Pooh was obese, lazy and illiterate. William Brown was in most respects worse. As for Alice, the object of Lewis Carroll's infatuation, she would have taken sweets from any stranger. Confronted by a bottle inscribed 'DRINK ME', Alice resisted the temptation only momentarily. After tasting it – 'it had . . . a sort of mixed flavour of cherry-tart, custard, pineapple, roast turkey, toffy and hot buttered toast' – she promptly drank it.

It seems hardly surprising that after next swallowing a cake marked 'EAT ME' she started seeing caterpillars smoking hookah pipes, sitting on magic mushrooms. Alice in wonderland was desperately in need of moral guidance. And as for that young chalet maid, Snow White . . . How successive generations of British children have turned out as well as they have is to be marvelled at.

As it turned out, the film of The Adventures of Peter Rabbit *was delayed in favour of a six-part television series, and Frederick Warne announced in November 1991 'start of production of the first and definitive animated version of the Original Peter Rabbit Books,* The World of Peter Rabbit and Friends, *due for delivery in Autumn 1992'. The six half-hour programmes would be made by the same team, produced by John Coates and directed and written by Dianne Jackson. 'Budgeted at $9 million it is the most expensive animated series ever to come out of the United Kingdom.'*

The following is an extract adapted from the text of Beatrix Potter's Art *(Warne 1989), Anne Stevenson Hobbs' selection of paintings and drawings from the artist's wide range of subjects and styles.*

BEATRIX POTTER'S OTHER ART

ANNE STEVENSON HOBBS, 1989

REPETITION AND variety, the keynotes of nature, are also the keynotes of Beatrix Potter's art, especially outside 'the little books' which have overshadowed her other achievements. Repetition, because she continually returned to favourite themes, redrawing and recopying, endlessly attempting to capture the world about her; variety, because within her own limits that range of subjects and styles was as wide as her experience allowed.

'I can't invent, I only copy', Beatrix later claimed. Yet she never aped another artist's manner – but selected, digested and modified. In later life she continued to 'copy what she saw' according to her creed. The 'highest and lowest in nature' were 'both equally perfect', from the swill bucket to the Lakeland hills whose watery atmosphere had captivated so many artists before her. Whatever the subject, she tackled it with professional detachment: 'I see no reason why common-sense should not foster a healthier appreciation of beauty than morbid sentimentality.'

Associated in the public imagination with one style, she experimented with medium, technique and scale. The 'miniaturist' painted spiders and fungi ten times larger than her vignettes. The practitioner of naturalism and precise detail played with broad washes and a palette of bright primaries. The investigative scientist used her knowledge with wit. The discipline of the camera and the microscope guided her vision, but she had, in her own words, the 'seeing eye': a memory both for places and for the sentiments they evoked. From ordinary, everyday objects she created a microcosm

135

of the world. She painted and drew to please herself, believing 'the more spontaneous the pleasure, the more happy the result'.

'It is all the same, drawing, painting, modelling, the irresistible desire to copy any beautiful object which strikes the eye. Why cannot one be content to look at it? I cannot rest, I must draw, however poor the result . . .'

All her life, observation inspired experimentation. She could look at similar subjects in different ways and tackle them in varying styles and techniques. Predating and partly coexisting with the bold chalk drawings and fluid pen-and-wash studies, her pointillistic stipple method (sometimes achieved by laying flat or shaded washes over minute dense pencil lines) made possible a virtuoso rendering of bloom and texture. In this she was influenced, as she admitted, by the Pre-Raphaelites. She could convey subtle and surprising differences of tone in hair or plumage, and the infinite gradations from light to dark. Minute subjects demanded minute strokes: with Bewick, William Hunt and Birket Foster, she is a descendant of the pictures 'in little' approach of the Elizabethans.

She makes one see, smell and touch what she paints, and has a sensuous awareness of the essential shape and feel of each object: crumbling leather and flaking rust, mould-encrusted branches, the crunchy dryness of seed-pods and papery rustle of onion skins – and the stiffness of a small dead fish with its accusing gelatinous eye. Her tactile sense is as insistent in the 'book pictures': a polished crab-apple; flowers embroidered in silk; the cold hard gleam of a dresser, redolent of beeswax; the highlighted lusciousness of a strawberry.

Except for her book pictures, she abandoned this miniaturist technique around 1900, adopting a bolder, more fluid line in pliable quill pen or brush. Line as well as colour inspired her to experiment. Her colour not only enhances the line; it models. The line itself sometimes becomes unobtrusive. The muted palette of her commercial work was dictated by the demands of chromolithography. Intensity returned with the sumptuous greens and flaming reds of parrot and toadstool, and denser, darker hues for dead blackbird

and furry spider. 'Grisaille', a technique of minute greyish-white brushstrokes producing a striking sculptural effect, was a natural progression from her exploration of the versatility of pencil; it had more three-dimensional possibilities. She painted 'Mr Pricklepin' with vivid multi-hued brushstrokes, an experiment extended further for sheep's heads in a looser pointillism and an even brighter palette.

Later, more adventurous colour work, in a style few would associate with 'Beatrix Potter', reflects an awareness of contemporary trends. A dash of colour may act as a focal point, sometimes doubling as light source (a candle, an open doorway, a glowing fire), sometimes in drawings which otherwise depend on line. Moonlight reflected on swirling water, the play of light on polished surfaces – all are instances of her fascination with the effects of light and shade.

Colour work later became an effort; Beatrix blamed the deterioration of her eyesight on the microscopic work and fungus drawing, but her housekeeper blamed it on working late by candlelight at Hill Top. Many of her last paintings – *Peter Rabbit* recopied to make money for the preservation of Windermere, the *Fairy Caravan* colour plates – are sadly pallid, or garish. What her paintings lost in detail they made up for in dynamism, as is shown by the mature versions of some *Appley Dapply* designs (1917), redrawn from her stippled 1890s originals.

The merest scraps of informal sketches show her flair for pictorial composition. She had definite ideas about the visual relationship of picture to text, liking to dictate the layout of her books, and making up her own dummies, cleverly using italics or white space for dramatic effect. Her occasional choice of framed illustrations as opposed to vignettes was intentional. Illustrations with edges needed borders: 'the black frame pulls them together & sends back the distance.' Endpapers should rest the eye, 'like a plain mount for a framed drawing'. Her modish round or oval vignettes set off the forms they enclose – a hollow forest glade, the flattened arch of a cart. Another compositional device is the rising or receding zigzag, which breaks up the picture and increases the sense of recession and depth. One's eye is coaxed not inwards but up and outwards, 'over the hills and far away'.

Imagining an animal's perspective, she portrays the creatures large in relation to their backgrounds. Samuel Whiskers on the landing is seen from cat height; the Puddle-ducks of Sawrey, higher than the viewer, gain in self-importance. The viewpoint can be a curious one. Parts of the picture may even dash off the page; centrifugal movement is accelerated when a peaceful clustering of mice turns into scampering mayhem.

In 1920 Beatrix wrote: 'It seems a pity . . . that some of my miscellaneous drawings cannot be published.' Those 'miscellaneous draw-ings' reveal the catholicity of an ardent observer. A brief survey of her themes indicates their relative importance: over five hundred

botanical studies but only a handful of figures.

Flowers and fruit had been an obvious and conventional choice; they reappear in her Tales. Next came gardens, from the precise formality of a tree-lined path by the Tay to the box edging at Gwaynynog and the Fawe Park backgrounds for *Benjamin Bunny*. Her Sawrey gardens, celebrated in *The Pie and The Patty-Pan* and *Tom Kitten*, have a Gertrude Jekyll lushness. Trees, the subject of letters, articles and fairy tales, intrigued her both scientifically and imaginatively. '*In the right place*' trees are 'as beautiful as rocks, and they have a nobility of growth which is usually intirely [*sic*] over looked.'

Her fungi are mostly shown in their natural settings, nestling among pine-needles and dry leaves, squatting in lichen and moss, or profiled among stiff grasses, in the tradition of Dürer's *The Great Piece of Turf*. It took two generations for Beatrix Potter's botanical illustrations to be valued as they deserved, and her pioneering discoveries were not acknowledged for sixty years. Today leading mycologists have at last begun to appraise both discoveries and drawings.

The handful of fossil studies ranks with her best work, as do the archaeological paintings of Roman artefacts from excavations in the City of London, exquisite in drawing and composition: a spiky pattern of nails, or a delicate tracery of needles and toilet utensils laid out like regimented spillikins.

Good design, and 'that appreciation of the fitness of things which is the soul of artistic taste', were important to Beatrix in all the arts – in architecture, textiles, dress and furniture. More than a hobby, furniture collecting became a mission. She wrote informed notes on carved oak, and secured good pieces for her Lake District farms. A particular piece of furniture inhabits a particular space. Beatrix recorded rooms wherever she stayed: the drawings were not just run-of-the-mill mementos. Staircases, passageways and empty attics provided useful exercises in perspective; a doorway some-times served as a frame.

Following the nostalgia of her time for roots and rusticity, she

139

became drawn to North Country vernacular. In these cottage kitchens, conviviality seems always in preparation if not in progress. The same snug cosiness pervades her more authentic settings. Safe burrows are hinted at behind hedgehog and vole or actually pictured from inside. It is a temporary safety only, contradicted by the alert ears and the little wild eyes. Outside is a cruel and uncosy world of murderous gardeners, foxes and wolves.

'What she instinctively felt about spaces – that they should be comforting, responsive and protective – was part of a general realization about spaces common to artists', writes Alison Smithson. '. . . Beatrix Potter succeeded in portraying forms entirely suitable for their purpose . . .' Equally suited to its purpose, and inseparable from its landscape, is the indigenous architecture of the Lake District, which became part of the fabric of her books. Architecture interested her from a young age. Her fairy stories have medieval backdrops; familiar houses, drawn also in their own right, supply backgrounds for her Tales. In *The Tailor of Gloucester*, the only book in the series with a period setting, all her interests come together: architecture and furniture, china and clothes.

Landscapes too appear in the early sketchbooks, dating from 1875–76. The composition improved with her photographic skills,

and in the 1890s she submitted landscapes to a small Drawing Society. The titles, so typical of a period when literature and art in England were closely linked, are often tags of poetry (especially Goldsmith and Gray). Maritime subjects and harbours were part of the English artist's repertoire. *The Tale of Little Pig Robinson* was an amalgam of Lyme Regis and its local thatch, Ilfracombe, Teignmouth shipping and the net sheds of Hastings. 'So the illustrations are a comprehensive sample of our much battered coasts.'

Where necessary, Beatrix resorted to artistic licence to 'improve' the composition, bending both the rules of naturalism and the arrangements of geology. Apart from such occasional leanings to the Picturesque, her places are actual rather than ideal. As she began to spend more time in the Lake District, she sketched by Windermere and her favourite Esthwaite Water, which she drew at every season and in every mood, most happily in its wintry aspect.

Like Helen Allingham, Beatrix Potter has been called a 'fair-weather painter'. The smiling landscapes of the Tales may give this impression – but there is plenty of weather in her watercolour sketches: 'Spring' at Harescombe Grange is balanced by 'Rain' at Lingholm, with its damp slates and sodden sky; ' A November Day' is reminiscent of Whistler. Some atmospheric effects, not unlike Ruskin's cloud formations, are a reminder too of her lifelong respect for Turner. A group of snow scenes dates from March 1909, and some little-known summer sketches survive from this period, done at speed in blobs of melting colour. These daringly impressionistic, almost abstract wash landscapes recall the late Wilson Steer. Quick sketches tend to look avant-garde in comparison with finished work; even so, these studies seem startlingly modern.

Amateurs, usually behind the times, make little progress through their careers – but Beatrix Potter was more than an amateur. As she wrote to Delmar Banner, artists move on, leaving behind the 'topographically-exact-in-detail' stage. Her diversity of styles was caused not just by deteriorating eyesight, but by a changing inner vision.

The name Beatrix Potter brings to mind not landscapes but figures in a landscape. The figures are usually animal ones, but playing their parts like humans. Landscape backgrounds are redrawn with figures skilfully placed. The scenery is much more than a backdrop, and even in the best compositions the figures need their landscapes more than the landscape needs figures. Human intrusion was avoided, and she found human anatomy 'a terrible bother'. Perhaps the mystique attached to life-drawing made her self-conscious, or perhaps she tried too hard, since her dashed-off figure sketches and the picture-letter stick people have plenty of life.

Human beings reminded her of animals, and 'a few of the animals were harmless skits or caricatures'. The creatures themselves are treated with affection and respect: they behave in character while satirizing human foibles and mannerisms: the confidence trickster wolf, his paws crossed in apparent relaxation, Tom Kitten's dumb insolence, Jemima's sheer silliness. The body language is half-human; the bodies are not.

Even in the nursery she had observed the behaviour of her pet animals as well as their anatomy – their resting and running positions, their hibernating and breathing patterns. Understanding both skeletal structure and musculature, she was well equipped to draw animals in all their grace and power, and did so with a detached but loving realism. Her microscopic work in particular was both appealing and accurate. Beetles, butterflies and moth wings, water creatures, claws and feet were compared at different angles and magnifications, often with the scale noted. Her scientific studies metamorphosed into imagined characters. The invertebrates and insects, amphibians and reptiles provide supporting cast and local colour: a snail on the wall, a fly on the doll's-house roof, a whole *corps de ballet* of butterflies, beetles and bees in *The Tale of Mrs. Tittlemouse*. Rabbits inspired an exceptional number of drawings, but mice populate the early rhyme pictures; she pictured them as busy and active, spinning or even stealing. Sheet after sheet is filled with studies, of several animals, of one animal, or of one particularly arresting feature: the translucent ears of mice and bats; the heads of rabbits and pigs.

Parody – sometimes tongue-in-cheek, sometimes concealed – was irresistible. Peter Rabbit at the door is a sly reflection of Anna Lea Merritt's *Love Locked Out* (1889). Duchess on the sofa mimics Briton Rivière's *Cupboard Love*. She pays her respects to Tenniel's sheep in

Little Pig Robinson, the *Tailor of Gloucester* frontispiece is a rather bland adaptation from Hogarth's *Times of the Day*, and Jemima Puddle-duck, with updated bonnet and shawl, has waddled straight out of a folk-tale illustration by Otto Speckter. Beatrix Potter seems to challenge her audience to find her out – courting discovery.

Away from the books and the fantasy pictures such subterfuge is redundant. The artist is herself challenged by her subject. The strongest subjects demand portrait treatment. In convenient repose they seem even more arresting: minute spiders, spreadeagled over her largest sheets, deceptively enlarged by the microscope; the bat, the weasel and the parrot, momentarily frozen yet wary-eyed; the skulls, eyeless but equally emphatic; and, glazed and sightless, the ram's mask, the crisply profiled orange fish, and the tragic stag, sprawled in the abandon of death. Long since stuffed, newly deceased or just resting, her animals have as glossy a presence as her fungi, which celebrate a decay teeming with new life.

Death and sleep are recurring themes in Victorian art, sleep and dream in Beatrix Potter's art. Rabbits lie on hearthrugs or in boxes, or like the mice are tucked up in brass bedsteads. Less comfortably, shadowy mood-paintings, moon- or candle-lit, can suggest oppression and even nightmare: a long panelled corridor, a wood from fairy tale. In the nocturnes of her late books one senses unease, loneliness and fear.

A sense of mystery never left her, nor did an underlying melancholy. Anxiety, vulnerability and pathos are implicit in the attitudes of her animals, belied by the outward serenity of her sunlit paintings. Always understated, never obvious, her pictures like her texts have hidden resonances; they are suffused with emotion and atmosphere. Through a subtle combination of composition, light and colour, more senses than sight are stimulated – the feel of smooth slate or dry leaves, the taste and smell of fog and frost, the unheard airs which accompany her dancing line.

Rosemary Wells is the writer and illustrator of many award-winning books for children. Through the preparation of the illustrations for her own books and through her work as a designer for a New York publisher she is used to seeing original artwork, but when she saw Beatrix Potter's watercolours she was overwhelmed.

SITTING IN HER CHAIR

ROSEMARY WELLS, 1991

BEATRIX POTTER was as great a painter as Turner or Reynolds but is not considered quite in their class because she was a woman and her painting was for children's books, of course.

Her work has been imitated, porcelained, choreographed, chopped up and completely redone. But once you open the little books nothing changes. I can use these books as a time-warp for myself. They take me into two worlds.

The first world is my own. It is a room that doesn't exist anymore. It was my bedroom when I was six and ten, fourteen and after. I am there at any of those ages with some mild illness good enough to keep me out of school. The wallpaper is light blue floral. The bed shoots away from the wall if I lean back too heavily. Drawn against my bed is a chintz-covered armchair which is where my dog is supposed to sleep but does not. She sleeps under the covers with me.

My mother puts me into bed, brings me aspirin and cocoa and I get every one of the little books off my shelves and read them all one after another. I see them now, scattered on the sides of the blanket mountain I make with my knees, bound in brown or bluish-grey paper.

As a child, I don't have any idea that I will be an illustrator, myself, one day. I would not dare to dream of being a published writer. The fact that any of this could be paid work would be too dizzying to contemplate. I do know I am an artist and will one day be a 'real one', although this fuzzes up into a future somehow involving oil paint. Oil paint to (non-musical) me is about as comforting as the violin.

Entering *her* world is what I do then and every time I pick up her books. It is never a syrupy land as some people believe a village of talking animals ought to be. It is more dignified and orderly than our own. It is one that exists as a parallel universe to life on planet earth. Children can step into that parallel universe as easily as they can step onto the balcony. Almost all adults have lost the key. But she could do it any old time. Fortunately for me I can still go there without a ticket or passport.

Last year I decided that in my own work I had invented many a funny character and many a universal dilemma of childhood, but I still had not created a world, as she did, as Hugh Lofting did, as Garth Williams has done. The reason for this was that I had honed my writing skills like mad and lazily loped along as an artist. It was time to go to work.

Art school in the sixties had taught me precious little technique. The faculty seemed to care only for Joseph Albers and his colored squares. The word 'Illustrator' was used in the pejorative sense. All of us who could draw well were secretly appalled. Inwardly we steamed, hating abstract expressionism, pretending to appreciate it, and terrified that at twenty years old we were on the cusp of the past.

At the age of forty-eight I decided to learn something about watercolor because I wanted at last to be a real artist. Also I had given myself three little manuscripts called 'Voyage to the Bunny Planet'. If I did not do these stories justice I knew I would never again be given anything as good (by the invisible hand in the sky that distributes ideas).

I went to England. Through the generosity of Anne Hobbs at the Victoria and Albert Museum, and Sally Floyer at Frederick Warne, I was able to sit with Jeremy Fisher and Samuel Whiskers on my lap and drink in all the secrets my eyes could find.

The first secret I found was that Beatrix Potter made mistakes like any normal artist. She whited them out with white paint so that the camera wouldn't 'see' them. Because her paper has faded and dulled, the white paint stands out now as it did not eighty or ninety years ago when she applied it.

At times she tried splicing. There is a drawing in the V & A archives the spit and image of the final art in *The Roly-Poly Pudding* where Tabitha Twitchit is mewing on the stairs beside a cherry velvet curtain. Tabitha's head is spliced on. So are several others threaded through the books.

An artist splices because of exhaustion. You get just to the point of perfection in a drawing that has taken hours and hours to complete. Perhaps you've drawn it six times. At the last minute you put down some line or splotch which isn't right. The drawing is ruined. You are fit to throw teacups at the wall. So instead of spending all that time redoing the whole drawing, you just redo the ruined part (usually it is a head and face) on another piece of paper over the light-table.

Get it right this time! Painstakingly you cut it out with a brand new blade. Then you have to cut a kiss-perfect matching shape out of the existing drawing. You winkle the new 'patch' into the hole which you think you've cut precisely to match but never matches. Then you spend hours with gouache (which is an opaque water-color) trying to obscure the cut lines with layer after layer of almost identical colors. All of this may take as long as the whole original drawing.

It almost never works right. Splicing is the hardest thing in all watercolor to do. It is rather like micro-surgery without the microscope. Once it is done it is unsatisfactory and you go back to a new piece of paper. You do the whole drawing over and discover that this takes a quarter of the time the splicing process did. The whole thing is better in inumerable little ways than the first one anyway, and then you ask yourself why you bothered with that stupid splice in the first place and you drop the spliced drawing in your box of 'maybe-keeps'.

I know she didn't have a light-box to trace her own work on. She probably held two pieces of paper against a window pane in the sun. Same thing. When I saw splicing in her work I laughed with recognition. It was rather like seeing the President at the dentist's office.

From that point on Anne Hobbs and I went over more than a hundred sketches, original book pieces and free-wheeling land-scapes. This is what I saw.

She worked in bad light a lot of the time. The strain on her eyes must have been enormous. A present-day artist must work in at least 200 watts of light. Neither the electric wiring nor bulbs available would have provided her that. She, like all painters of her time and before, worked in conditions that would cramp and exasperate a modern painter, accustomed as we are to lumbar-support chairs, easily-tilting drawing-boards, and instant access to art supply stores with their fabulous array of materials at any hour of the work week. If she ran out of a color, or paper or split her last nib hopelessly, it would have required considerable time and journey to replace anything, and so she made do with blunt pens and tired brushes. I was left with a distinct impression of how she worked. It was something close to Escoffier concocting a feast for royalty in the kitchen of a house trailer and not minding a bit. Beatrix Potter could do more with a five-year-old camel-hair brush than any of us today could do with enough sable brushes to line a coat.

The degree of light available outdoors where she painted her lovely wet into wet landscapes of downs and moors was much greater. Here the shapes have quicker moving masses of color because she could see better. She bought inexpensive paper (alas full of time-released acids), probably at a village stationers. Some of what she used was Bristol, good stock for the times, but she did not use French rag papers which would have lasted and remained white for donkey's years.

I became so deeply aware of what colors she was using on different drawings that I could fairly see her palette (heavy on sap green, Antwerp blue, gamboge and mauve). When I spend seven or eight hours a day mixing paints and flicking from color to color (and there are a finite number of real colors), I then go for a walk in the woods and every blade of grass is a shade of Hooker's or viridian green. Every leaf is a wash of burnt sienna and Van Dyke brown. To my eye her colors are easily recognized. She used very good quality pigments – probably Winsor & Newton artist's grade. She may have mixed some of her own, using pure pigment and gum arabic. This is evident because although her paper hasn't lasted well her colors have remained quite brilliant.

She started most drawings in pencil, erased it after a first inking and sometimes erased a little too vigorously on this nasty stock where the surface rubs off easily. For ink-line work she used a very flexible long nib (not a crow quill). Often her line is done in brush. Brush-line runs very nicely and is not subject to sudden catches and squiffs. Her most successful and lovely line is done in sepia ink. Probably the same as sold today at Cornelissen's opposite the British Museum. They still carry a French sepia ink which clots beautifully and is as flexible off the pen as mercury. I bought six bottles of it on my last London visit. Almost all her studies of leaves and plants are done with this sepia. It flows better than black India ink, for one reason – it does not dry up, crab and thicken in its bottle.

She had trouble drawing people. They didn't come easily through her hand. (I use the word *through* because when an idea courses from the netherworld into an artist's mind, it comes out of the hand. Whether the hand is on the keys of a piano, holding a brush, a baton or pecking on a typewriter, it is all the same. Ideas come from somewhere in the cosmos, nobody knows, but it is from the outside.) People were sticky for her. She was not comfortable with their size or proportions. What sings, in so many of her pictures, is a great love of hedgerows, rams, dogs, ducks, mice and blackberries, anything that grew and prospered in God's world except for human beings, and she undoubtedly had good reason for these preferences. There is an awkwardness with her people's bodies and faces as if the idea of them came through her fingers stiffly and without some vital information about them.

It was as well. Her stories are almost entirely about animals anyway. People are incidental to the great body of her work. While 'sitting in her chair', with her drawings fresh as the day they were done in my lap, I began to feel her presence as if she were standing there next to me.

I believe she never took herself too seriously or her work too lightly. I believe she hungered for the robustness and earthiness of animals, meadows and the wildness of tiny things in the woods. In direct opposition to citified Freudian dogma, I believe she saw great sensuousness in hedgerows and in streams. I think she found people wooden and repressive because that is how she drew them.

Deep in the drawings of Peter Rabbit and Squirrel Nutkin is what she was to become. It is all there to be read in the cold water of her tarns and the soft English shadows of her farm scenes. Her life's greatest happiness was to be found at last in breeding and judging sheep; in managing a farm, long after the books were complete. It is tempting to say that such rough ordinary chores were somehow *less* than her work as an artist. Instead they were a logical extension.

When I first learned that she had set her painting and books aside rather early in life, I was disappointed, wishing she had done more. Now I understand that her farmer's calling was as great a work as the twenty-three books she wrote and illustrated. Her legacy left a part of England painfully beautiful, the way it was in the best of its times. It allowed me, an American visitor, born the year she died, to walk on hillsides unspoiled by human greed of any kind.

I believe that her books were an explosion out of a tiny cramped room of her childhood. When they were done, she had the graciousness never to milk the cosmos for more.

Beatrix Potter was as marvelous an artist as Turner or Reynolds. The essence of her genius in a painted vision is not only that one can see so much as that one can hear. Listening to her landscapes I hear the leaves patter under the Cumbrian rain, the distant lowing of cows at milking time. I hear something else, too, and it is distinctly American (a people I am proud to say she liked). I hear the voice of an artist quite close to her in spirit. It is the voice of America's greatest poet, Robert Frost.

> He gives his harness bells a shake
> To ask if there is some mistake.
> The only other sound's the sweep
> Of easy wind and downy flake.

As the characters from the little books are increasingly the inspiration for cartoons in magazines and newspapers across the world, I asked Nicholas Garland about his particularly ingenious use of them in his political cartoons.

'CONTROLLED WOOL-GATHERING': THE POLITICAL CARTOONIST AND BEATRIX POTTER

NICHOLAS GARLAND, 1991

ONE OF THE questions cartoonists are most frequently asked is, 'How do you get your ideas?' The truth is that cartoonists do not know exactly where their ideas come from – and that is why our job is so very difficult. Drawing up an idea is nothing compared to thinking it up in the first place.

The process of creating a cartoon involves taking in information, thinking logically about it and then deciding on a point of view or attitude to express. But at a certain moment you must begin to free associate your thoughts, to allow your mind to go off at tangents, to go in for a bit of controlled wool-gathering. At this point it is still uncertain whether a cartoon idea will emerge or not. What you are searching for is a scene that will act as a vehicle for the notion or attitude you want to convey.

There are many situations from literature, mythology and history that lodge in everyone's minds as encapsulated fragments of the human condition. They serve as a kind of shorthand in conversation – and in cartooning. For example, 'turning a blind eye' is so much part of the language that we hardly bother to remember the superbly confident Lord Nelson who gave us the phrase. A cartoonist wishing to show a politician ignoring the inevitable, and possibly disagreeable, consequences of a decision has only to draw the man clapping a telescope to an eye patch and the job is done.

It is possible to draw up quite a long list of these references with which any educated person will be familiar. Such a list includes most of *Alice* (the Cheshire Cat frequently appears in political cartoons), a lot of Shakespeare ('To be, or not to be', etc.), much Greek and Roman mythology (Icarus, Narcissus, Medusa, for example). Then there are the advertising slogans ('My Goodness, My Guinness') and scores of nursery rhymes and children's stories.

Beatrix Potter's tales are filled with scenes and characters that can be used by the cartoonist. In her case the situations come with inexpressably charming and witty illustrations which it is a delight to parody.

The Story of A Fierce Bad Rabbit fits the actions of any number of politicians making trouble in their parties by seizing the initiative (the carrot) from their leaders or colleagues. Daffy Jemima Puddle-Duck is a marvellous example of self-destructive gullibility. *The Story of Miss Moppet* is a solid pile of political cartoons waiting to happen. As for *The Tale of Two Bad Mice*, open the book at random and almost every spread provides a source for inspiration.

'Tom Thumb set to work at once to carve the ham. It was a beautiful shiny yellow, streaked with red. The knife crumpled up and hurt him . . . .' A politician trying to change a situation, to cut it down to size or to cut into it. But it is too hard; the lead knife bends in his hand.

Look at the picture of Tom Thumb and Hunca Munca pulling the feathers out of Lucinda's bolster: one male and one female politician, feeling that their party is not being right-wing enough, 'set to work to do all the mischief they could' by shredding its policy on Europe.

'There were two red lobsters and a ham, a fish, a pudding, and some pears and oranges. They would not come off the plates, but they were extremely beautiful.' An obvious choice for a cartoon about something that looks good but is in fact useless.

There is a school of cartooning that relies on creating grotesque and violently distorted representations of politicians. Making use of Beatrix Potter's books as vehicles for cartoons is to discover a gentler mode. Her style is comic and lends itself to irony and

good-natured mockery rather than to outraged abuse. Mockery can be far more subversive and difficult to handle than any amount of invective.

"NUTKIN BECAME MORE AND MORE IMPERTINENT ... BUT STILL OLD BROWN SAID NOTHING AT ALL,"
(THE TALE OF SQUIRREL NUTKIN)

153

Brian Alderson presented one of the seven papers at the first Beatrix Potter Society Conference held in the Lake District in July 1984, when his subject was 'Beatrix Potter – The Writer'. Earlier that year he had given the Fourth Linder Memorial Lecture to the Society, 'Peter Rabbit in his Time', an account of the state of publishing and the book trade when Beatrix Potter was seeking a publisher for The Tale of Peter Rabbit. *Now he turns his attention to the history of the merchandise featuring the Potter characters.*

'ALL THE LITTLE SIDE SHOWS': BEATRIX POTTER AMONG THE TRADESMEN

BRIAN ALDERSON, 1992

FROM THE START of their history as a commercial product, children's books have had a place in the cluttered world of nursery accessories. When Mary Cooper, one of the founders of the trade, published *The Child's New Plaything* round about 1743 she bound into it a fold-out engraving of an alphabet which could be cut up and used as a guessing game. And her energetic competitor, John Newbery, not only seems to have quickly copied this device with a game (now lost) called 'Who Will Play at my Squares' but – typically – brought in new ploys of his own. One of his earliest children's books, the famous *Little Pretty Pocket-Book* of *c.* 1744, could be sold with a ball or pincushion the use of which, buyers were assured, 'will infallibly make Tommy a good boy and Polly a good girl'. They cost two-pence each.

As trade expanded and the market grew more reliable and more eager for novelties the range of goods associated with children's books diversified. At the end of the eighteenth century great play was made with single engraved sheets, illustrated and often hand-coloured, and put to multiple use. A sheet could be folded up into a

154

book or mounted on thin strips of mahogany and cut up as a jigsaw. Adventurous figures like John Bunyan's Pilgrim or Cowper's John Gilpin, who had found their way into the nursery, had their careers reduced to a single set of pictures which could be hung on a wall or, again, folded to make a picture book. Even the redoubtable Mrs Trimmer, the 'guardian of education', got in on the act. The prints that adorned her various historical synopses ('Ancient History', 'Roman History', etc.) were also available in sheet form, mounted for hanging on the schoolroom walls.

Individuals like Pilgrim and Gilpin and Mr Punch (who came in to literature from outside) were, I suppose, the first fictional characters to be exploited in a number of products which used their household popularity as a means to commercial appeal. John Gilpin, for instance, quickly became a subject for the makers of ceramics and decorative prints. The first genuine characters from children's literature itself, though, who found their way into other parts of the market may well have been Struwwelpeter, who leapt to fame throughout Europe soon after his first appearance at Frankfurt in 1845, and Lewis Carroll's Alice, who, with attendant white rabbits, mad hatters and Cheshire Cats, has inspired everyone from playing-card designers to the manufacturers of biscuit tins. (Different in kind, but perhaps more pervasive, were the dream-children invented by Kate Greenaway – lacking all individuality, but bringing a parade of mob-caps, pinafores and button-breeches into every quarter of commercial and decorative art.)

Thus, when Beatrix Potter sat down in December 1903 to make a Peter Rabbit doll she was doing no more than enter a tradition that was already long established. She may have been prompted in part by the challenge of the thing – fashioning a look-alike three-dimensional Peter – and also by a wish to make a present for Fruing Warne's daughter Winifred, but she soon discovered that there was 'a run on toys copied from pictures' and realized that she would do well to safeguard her proprietorship in the characters in her books. Harrods were casting a predatory eye on rabbits; her father had bought a squirrel called 'Nutkin' in the Burlington Arcade; so without more ado she registered her doll at the Patent Office – the first step in the industrialization of the little books.

If she had not sensed the potential of book-based merchandise when she worked on Peter, only a few months would elapse before the implications became pretty clear. In October 1904 she writes to her publishers that she has heard from a distant acquaintance, a Mrs Garnett, who 'has made a frieze for her nursery out of Peter Rabbit' and who ('rather cool') is inquiring about getting it made commercially. A muted but insistent buzzing of alarm bells can be heard. Can Mrs Garnett draw? (Later it turns out that her pictures are 'ludicrously bad'.) Will she drop the idea when she realizes that Warne will exact a royalty? The sales potential of a frieze may well be considerable, but should not the designing be done by Beatrix Potter herself 'if it were not too much trouble'? 'The idea of rooms covered with badly drawn rabbits is appalling . . .'

Mrs Garnett proved to be 'pertinaceous' as well as not very competent, but the upshot of her intrusion on the scene was that Beatrix Potter went out and 'discovered another lady – Mrs Spicer – who has had experience in the work' of wallpaper designing, and between the two of them they 'disposed of' Mrs Garnett and created a frieze which eventually went into production. The designing was a heavy job, but not unsuccessful. 'We have done them flat, like stencil colours; they are less frightful than might have been expected, and Mr McGregor is magnificent on the frieze.'

From this time onward, for almost twenty-five years, the devising of products related to her work, or the negotiation of contracts and the discussion of manufacturing procedures became a regular feature of Beatrix Potter's business life. While the wallpaper fuss was rumbling along (and while she was also drafting *Mrs. Tiggy-Winkle*, *Jeremy Fisher* and *The Pie and The Patty-Pan*) she found time to plan 'The Game of Peter Rabbit', complete with a full

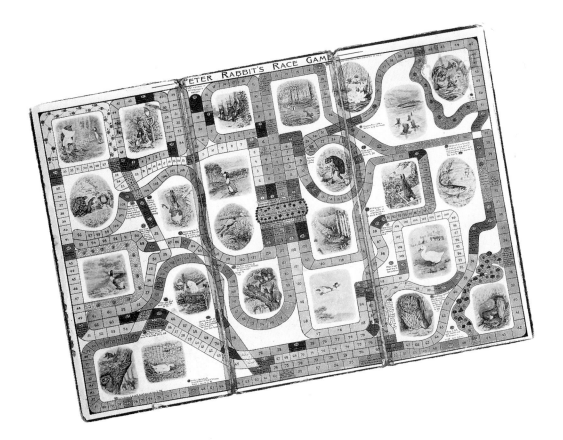

sketch of the playing board and a detailed set of rules. A year or two later, the ceramics industry became interested in using her pictures on nursery chinaware and agreements were set in train. Although the First World War interrupted the smooth progress of events, once it was over a whole string of goods with Potter associations were contemplated or authorized by herself and her publisher.

The first of these, the Peter Rabbit handkerchiefs, had actually come on the market in 1917 and were pronounced 'wonderful' by Beatrix Potter. 'I feel sure they will have a good sale – of course the stitching at that price of 6d each must have limitations, but the boxes alone are enough to sell it.' (Within a year 1,500 boxes had gone off and only shortages of labour were impeding greater production.) Wall pictures and children's slippers were to follow in

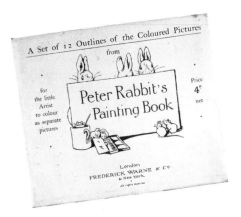

1919. Baby goods, like a crawling-rug and a feeder, were mooted in the twenties, and there were various productions more closely related to the published books: book-ends, a bookcase to take a complete set of the stories, and adaptations of the books themselves for such ephemeral publications as painting books, stencils, calendars and Christmas cards.

Correspondence, published and unpublished, reveals the extent, and sometimes the complexity, of these fringe activities which Beatrix Potter, in a letter to Harold Warne, once referred to as 'all the little side shows'. Some schemes went through smoothly or provoked only brief discussion – the 'Peter Rabbit Race Game', for instance, may have hung fire for twelve years, but when it did emerge in a design by her publisher's wife, Mary Warne, the author accepted that the new version was probably more marketable than her own and the game went on to be a success that has lasted to this day.

With the dolls and the chinaware, however, complications abounded and, so far as the dolls were concerned, brought no very tangible reward. Beatrix Potter's efforts to market the Peter Rabbit toy had been largely frustrated by a ceaseless flow of cheap rabbit dolls from Germany which could not easily be blocked by appeals to patent law and which totally inhibited English manufacturers from marketing a doll under licence. (This frustrating circumstance was one of the promptings behind 'the year when Bee went into politics' (1910), when she spent much time campaigning against Free Trade and its wrecking of the South London toy industry.) In

1904, though, a new set of negotiations had got under way over a Jemima Puddle-Duck doll which had been modelled by a Mrs Porter who ran a toy shop in Sussex Place, just off the Bayswater Road. Beatrix handled the matter herself – 'the only side show which I arranged personally and accounted for' – and found herself embroiled with 'grubby and depressed' tradesmen in places like Houndsditch on the other side of London.

Eventually a patent was registered and terms were arranged with Messrs J.K. Farnell, who manufactured mostly for the wholesale trade and who would pay a royalty of 5% to be split between author and publisher. This small percentage was partly due to the trading margins in novelty goods, which were much larger than those of the book trade. 'You will be shocked to hear,' wrote Beatrix Potter to Harold Warne in 1910, 'that the discount in the toy trade is 50%'; on the other hand, the sales of successful lines were measured in grosses rather than in humble dozens.

On the whole the arrangement worked well, producing a small regular return for a number of years, and Beatrix would have liked to extend the range of characters beyond the solitary Jemima. Farnell's, too, may have been interested, but plans look to have foundered owing to the dilatoriness of Harold Warne. With a letter, undated, but from about 1925, 'Beatrix Potter', as she subscribes herself, despatches 'a parcel of Farnell letters' which 'are not very satisfactory reading; and they bring back painful memories. H[arold] used to muddle sideshows, and turn me on to them when we were mutually out of temper . . .'. So a subsidiary operation that looked to have profitable possibilities came to very little.

The only other recorded attempt at doll-making in Beatrix's lifetime occurred round abut 1923 when the Chorley Rubber Company engaged with Warne to produce rubber figures of Peter Rabbit, Benjamin Bunny, Tom Kitten and Jemima Puddle-Duck. Beatrix Potter found these 'excellent', but the manufacturer seems to have been having a difficult time and nothing more was done. Only with the coming of modern processes and the use of synthetic materials has a concerted effort been made to capitalize on dolls.

So far as chinaware is concerned there again appear to have been some false starts. Before the First World War an agreement was made, probably with a German firm, to manufacture tea-sets. This would have gone much against Beatrix Potter's political instincts, and the contract was loosely worded anyway, there being no certainty as to whether it included earthenware (which she wanted to deal with separately in order to find someone to make statuettes). Moreover, she found the china 'very ugly', so in 1917 the agreement with the English agent who had initiated the original contract, Mr Levien, was terminated and a new start was made. Beatrix herself followed up a request from Grimwades Ltd of the Winton Potteries, Stoke-on-Trent, that they might model some figurines and also, in their words, make 'the lithographic reproduction of your Jemima Puddleduck and other similar subjects on articles for the nursery such as Baby Plates, Porridge Plates, Children's Mugs &c.'

Beatrix was anxious to proceed with some arrangement as soon as possible. 'Copyright actions are doubtful; the best protection is to get out authorized china' and in 1918 permission was given to Grimwades to proceed. But progress was cumbersome, with the author and publisher negotiating from two points of the compass on one side and with Grimwades apparently splitting production between a design studio and a manufacturing pottery at their end. At that period, too, there were difficulties over the use of labour and over the supply of materials, and the four-year agreement had eventually to be redated to commence in 1921. Even then there were failures in distribution. Beatrix Potter praised Grimwades' craftsmanship: the samples 'are beautifully done . . . if they can get on with them' she wrote in 1920; and, rather pointedly, in 1922: 'the china . . . is splendid – far better printed than modern editions of the books as regards true register', but most of the trade sales were made by the Warne travellers rather than by experienced pottery salesmen. This was not so much discouraging as frustrating, since the pottery was very well received and both author and publisher were – rightly – conscious of a large untapped retail market.

A systematic reading of the Potter–Warne correspondence on these side shows confirms what has already been generally accepted: that Beatrix Potter was not just motivated by a wish to protect her creations from mercantile piracy or to ensure that their adaptation to 'other purposes' was carried out according to her own exacting standards. She also very much relished the challenge of devising adaptations which would be good paying propositions, and she could be just as much amused as pained by silly submissions or by unconventional ideas. 'I don't see how you could possibly work a royalty on *biscuits*', she wrote in 1912 to her publisher, not forseeing the day when Woolworth would be selling tins of Beatrix Potter Peter Rabbit Cookies.

So far as the exploitation of Beatrix Potter's books themselves is concerned, their conversion into alternative printed versions is an aspect of merchandising which raises questions that have to do with textual criticism rather than with the commercial applications that I am considering here. Nevertheless, in one instance, a piratical swoop in the direction of doll-making led to the author becoming involved in some unusual negotiations about physical adaptation.

In 1909 the market-leaders in rag-book and novelty publishing, Thomas Dean & Sons, announced that they were going to produce a series of dolls 'as popularized by Beatrix Potter'. Warne, who had always been on friendly terms with the company, made formal objections and the matter was settled without going to court. Dean's, however, followed up this contact by suggesting a rag-book edition of *Peter Rabbit*, with a second, unnamed, Potter title to be 'remodelled in abbreviated form'. Options were open, and rough samples with some illustrations 'redrawn . . . for flat colour' were despatched to Sawrey for the author's opinion, coupled with the tempting information that editions of 8,000 of each title would be published at the usual royalty.

The author replied with remarkable tolerance: 'I should say it is worth doing . . . It seems a bit dog-in-the-manger to stop them altogether', and she not only thought that 'the flat colours work out wonderfully well', but made some constructive suggestions on how to 'compress Peter to the smaller size', remarking unconcernedly, 'I should say cut down the story pretty hard'.

The incident is a tribute to Beatrix Potter's pragmatism, revealed both in her appreciation of the adapted illustrations (compare her remarks on the wallpaper frieze of 1905) and in her willingness to reduce the number of words in the story – which is a practicality that she had recognized ever since the tailored trade edition of *The Tailor of Gloucester*. Furthermore, her interest in the project (which ultimately came to naught) was conditioned by her awareness that all matters concerning the editing and production of the rag-books would have to be agreed by her. Only the legendary optimism of publishers could interpret this show of adaptability as an indirect sanction of the 'V. Andal-ized' texts about which Rumer Godden wrote so feelingly (see page 83), or for the distortions of the stories that occurred so famously in the editions published by Frederick Warne's sister company, Ladybird Books, in 1987.

Central to that dispute, which concerned the *rewriting* of her texts, is what we understand by literary integrity: the acceptance and preservation of the author's work in the form closest to her own intentions. And a concern for literary integrity is what gives rise to unease about merchandising procedures – the sometimes crude exploitation of disparate parts of a 'text' for alternative purposes – no matter that history shows such commercial exploitation to be predictable and, in places, to follow a traditional pattern.

Thus, after the Second World War, Frederick Warne's list included adaptations like jig-saw puzzles, wall pictures, and the Race Game, which were unwitting repetitions of the ploys of the children's book merchandisers of the eighteenth century. At the same time, though, there seems to have been a growing awareness – sharpened up by faltering profits – that more could be made of the Potter properties. Leslie Linder's work, and especially the National Book League Centenary Exhibition of 1966 which he organized, mightily raised Beatrix Potter's popularity – but how could commercial sideshows be devised and expanded without undermining her own uncompromising standards?

Conscious of their responsibilities, Frederick Warne set up a committee to plan a more systematic approach to the licensing of Potter material and to advise on the suitability of projects that were suggested. Refinements in the laws relating to copyright and trade-mark protection were under way and during the late 1970s and early 1980s goods began to appear like the silk bookmarks 'by Cash's the Weavers of Coventry', or the eight jig-saws from 'Beatrix Potter Creations', which show a growing momentum in the adaptation of the little books to other purposes.

With the purchase of Warne by Penguin in 1983, this rather hesitant tinkering was replaced by a campaign that was clearly the result of much forethought and was conducted with near-military precision. Frederick Warne (Publishers) Ltd, 'the old firm', had already held preliminary negotiations with an agent, with the appropriate name of Copyrights Ltd, to administer the licensing of products based upon Beatrix Potter's *oeuvre*. Penguin Books completed the deal, and a systematic monitoring of products was instituted, with a two-way traffic in ideas. Companies submitted schemes for approval; Penguin and Copyrights spied out areas where the writ of Beatrix Potter might yet run.

In its planning and execution this campaign has been carried out with pragmatic flair (stimulated no doubt by the knowledge that Beatrix Potter would be 'entering the public domain' in 1994). Over 170 companies are now licensed to use some part of her work in dozens of varieties of merchandise, from nursery furniture to paper partyware, and from lavender-bags to hand-painted glass roundels. But whatever the goods, an obeisance is made to standards of reproduction, and a firm control is exercised to ensure that manufacturers hold to the quality of Beatrix Potter's original designs.

In the course of this expansion of trade, traditional concepts of appropriate relations between image and product, or of catering for a child market have also been dramatically widened. There are probably many licences issued these days for things like Earl Grey Tea tins or size 40 sweaters, in which children will make little imaginative investment, and the images on such goods frequently have only a tenuous relationship to their use, so that it is difficult to determine why a Potter image is being adopted at all. There might be some point in marketing a Fierce Bad Rabbit shot-gun or a Ginger and Pickles account book, but what does Jemima Puddle-duck have to do with pictorial soap or Tabitha Twitchit with fudge tins?

Several assumptions can be put forward as to why so much business acumen is being expended on recruiting the small creatures of Lakeland to the busy causes of World Trade. First and foremost is probably the fact simply of their winning personalities and appearance – that they are indeed just small creatures, dressed up funny, who can supply a bit of decorative cheer to otherwise humdrum goods. At the same time – and this will be variable – the images may carry with them some hint of associations that the promoter hopes will engender an amiable disposition among the customers. At best that may flow from happy recollections of books which adults encountered in childhood or which children are already encountering – a meeting with old friends known in other circumstances. At a lesser level there will simply be the recognition that these are 'Beatrix Potter characters', and thus part of some indefinable

English pastoral heritage of which it is pleasing to be reminded among the paraphernalia of our very un-pastoral times.

In all probability this appeal of a generalized 'World of Beatrix Potter' accounts for the limited use that has so far been made by manufacturers of the full range of images in her books. There are powerful marketing pressures to select emblems that are immediately identifiable, and it comes as no surprise that the most popular titles drawn upon for merchandise are, in descending order, *Peter Rabbit, Jemima Puddle-Duck, Benjamin Bunny, Mrs. Tiggy-Winkle* and *Tom Kitten*, with consolation prizes to *Jeremy Fisher* and *Squirrel Nutkin*. These are only seven books out of a total of more than twenty, and the images chosen for reproduction from their pages are also very limited. Probably the most popular from Beatrix Potter's time to the present are the watercolour of Peter running, from the cover of *Peter Rabbit*, the picture of Peter eating radishes, the group portrait of Mrs Rabbit bidding farewell to her family before going shopping and, perhaps, Jemima in one of her dafter poses and Benjamin Bunny in his tam-o'-shanter.

Sometimes, of course, ambitious attempts are made to extend the range. The Wedgwood children's china goes some way towards telling the whole story of Peter Rabbit, with the text transferred as well, moving from mug to bowl to plate to cup and saucer. What are known as 'the Beswick figures' comprehend a mighty array of characters, some represented several times in different postures (Jeremy Fisher, for instance, is to be found digging *and* sitting on his lily-pad). On the whole though, the persistent repetition of a small group of images is a regrettable and possibly a counter-productive ploy. It is regrettable because it has the effect of converting something that was once freshly imagined into a stale cliché. It is counter-productive because an image is being used that bears no relevance to the object that sports its favour.

From the publisher's point of view this may not be an ideal state of affairs, since the preconceptions of non-literary publicists may reflect the buying public's own limited awareness. The likelihood is that – merchandise or no merchandise – the print-runs of *The Tale of Peter Rabbit* or *The Tale of Jemima Puddle-Duck* will always be substantial; what may be needed is a few more entrepreneurs to focus on less immediately seductive titles like *The Tale of Timmy Tiptoes* and *The Pie and The Patty-Pan*, which might be good for the series as a whole. Certainly the current move towards giving more information about the stories behind characters featured on Potter products, and the selling of copies of individual books wrapped in with related hardware, shows a renewed awareness of priorities. If sales of a Ginger & Pickles Home Accounts Ledger were to widen the audience for that recondite narrative so much the better for the full comprehension of Beatrix Potter's art.

And such comprehension is of course what it would be nice to find in buyers of Beatrix Potter's merchandise. Few children will ever be able to collect Beswick figures at £12.95 or more a throw, but the fun of doing so would be to recognize each statuette in its own narrative moment, aware of the story that surrounds it. Many children will construct the 'Peter Rabbit Theatre', or play with the 'Peter Rabbit Race Game', and they will, as Beatrix Potter noted, get enjoyment or excitement from the exercise if they are 'fond of the book'.

A number of products of more ingenious design do in fact induce a more engaged response, in that they themselves play games with the characters and the stories. Beatrix Potter had no time for 'an objectionable woman' who turned up with some tea-cosies in 1926, but if she could have seen the Sari Product cosy of 1988 she would surely have been charmed. The thing is in the shape of the house at Hill Top, which forms a setting for a composite group of characters: Nutkin, Jeremy Fisher and Samuel Whiskers look out of the windows, and there are some visitors in the garden. These include Tabitha Twitchit and Tom Kitten, talking to Mrs Tiggy-Winkle in the doorway (substituting for the real owner), and Mrs Rabbit with her daughters, while Peter is squeezing under a gate.

There is nothing new in saying that 'the little books' add up to a wonderfully articulate whole – articulate in their storytelling and in the interconnections between characters and events that occur from book to book. (Perhaps that may have been realized – supplementary to plain, commercial thinking – when the first Beatrix Potter book-case was made.) Set beside her small, but almost perfect, achievement, the bandying about of a few fanciful excerpted pictures is of only marginal consequence, except to the participating tradesmen, unless it can direct attention to the wealth of imagery that waits to be explored. Making appeals to instant recognition or instant nostalgia is a limiting exercise.

But such unimaginative use of her work is perhaps a sign that Beatrix Potter will be protected by the very gap that exists between the overdone clichés and the obscurer pleasures. We cannot forecast what will happen after 1994, when texts will be razed and storybooks devastated (even though, apparently, much of Beatrix Potter's original artwork will continue to be protected by an astute use of trade-mark legislation). Nevertheless, the adaptors and the reillustrators will start their own sideshows and it will be instructive to see in which direction their commercial instincts take them. Peter Rabbit is already a lost cause, but Timmy Tiptoes may well escape, by virtue of his greater inaccessibility; and who is to say that the same will not apply to Mr Jackson, Aunt Pettitoes and those two nefarious characters last seen tumbling over the rocks on the side of Bull Banks.

'Collecting Beatrix Potter' has become a popular hobby for many enthusiasts, but finding – and affording – first editions of the little books is becoming increasingly difficult. The rare copies of her privately-printed The Tale of Peter Rabbit *fetch astronomical prices at auction and even copies of the first Warne editions of the titles cannot be found for much less than £100. Selwyn Goodacre has been a collector for many years, not of Potter first editions but of 'issues of the Hill Top Guide, Potter postage stamps and covers, catalogues, books and articles concerned with Beatrix Potter, and books written and illustrated by people closely connected with her'. He also specializes in Potter 'piracies'.*

'PETER RABBIT AND HIS MA': COLLECTING BEATRIX POTTER PIRACIES

SELWYN GOODACRE, 1991

I BEGAN COLLECTING children's books as a teenager, and for many years concentrated almost exclusively on Lewis Carroll. The field was open in those days, for there were few who were interested in gathering together hundreds of copies of the *Alice* books. In later years I 'diversified' into other children's authors, particularly those whose books I had enjoyed as a child. Beatrix Potter had always been a favourite and was an obvious choice, but I soon realized that others before me had mined the field very fully, and that it would be preferable to explore neglected areas of her work. A dealer listed a number of what he called 'Beatrix Potter Piracies'. I was hooked.

I use the word 'piracy' possibly a little loosely. For me it covers any edition of the Potter books not published under her direct sanction, or without her publisher's full acquiescence, or with the unauthorized use of the Peter Rabbit name. Strictly speaking piracy implies illegality but many of the editions discussed below *were* legal – though I feel that Potter herself would hardly have approved of them. As for the books that were published after her death, I concentrate on those publications I have encountered that stray from the author's original concept.

Trouble for the Potter books began right at the start. In 1904 Beatrix Potter's publishers, Frederick Warne, realized with some dismay that they had failed to register the copyright of *The Tale of Peter Rabbit* in the USA, and that a pirated edition was about to appear. Nothing could be done about it at that late stage, except to ensure that more care was taken in later years. The firm of Henry Altemus of Philadelphia, established in 1790, had moved into the juvenile book market in the 1890s, and by the turn of the century was producing vast numbers of popular classics. Their first pirated *Alice*s had appeared in 1895. It was inevitable that they should seize the chance to 'cash in' on the new best seller from England, where, by 1904, over 50,000 copies of *Peter Rabbit* had been sold.

Not appreciating that Potter and Warne were revising their own edition with virtually every print run, refining the text here and there, Altemus simply took up the latest edition available – the fourth printing, dated 1903, and used both text and pictures. Frozen in time as it were, the Altemus edition therefore included four pictures that were later to be dropped from the English edition in order to make way for the new coloured endpapers. Three of these are relatively unimportant (Peter running to the garden was already on the front cover), but the fourth is more significant, since it shows Mrs McGregor serving up Peter's father in the pie. Potter had tactfully omitted Mr McGregor relishing the prospect ahead (see page 132), but Altemus had no such inhibitions – Mr McGregor appears, grossly out of proportion, with knife and fork at the ready.

Whatever the morals of the situation, the Altemus edition of the book is nicely produced, apart from the rather lurid green cover. It is about the same size as the original edition, the pictures are reasonable copies, but with none of the delicate touch shown by Edmund Evans, the printer of the early Warne editions.

Inevitably the book was a success, and spawned a whole host of 'sequels'. For these, Altemus adopted a new style of cover: a paste-on picture, taken from the text of the sequel in question, is positioned below the title, with margins on either side. A vaguely pastoral scene is in the background. The sequels began to appear in about 1915 in certain well-defined groups. For each group, the list was headed by another issue of *The Tale of Peter Rabbit* which took on the style of the series (the front cover picture shows Peter having his coat put on). The quality of the pictures of this new *Peter* is a sad fall off from the (relatively) high standard of the first edition, the colours now mostly in undifferentiated blocks. The text for the first sequels for the first series – *How Peter Rabbit went to Sea* and *Peter Rabbit at the Farm* – were written by Duff Graham.

The next series introduced the prolific Linda Stevens Almond, who wrote over ten sequels, with titles as diverse as *Peter Rabbit went to School* and *Peter Rabbit and the Old Witch Woman*. Other authors added to the flood of titles. The books present problems bibliographically, for the series titles change ('Wee Books for Wee Folks', 'The Peter Rabbit Series', and so on), and copyright dates only are given rather than actual dates of printing. Lists of other titles in the series are usually included in advertisements at the end of the books. Minor variants in these adverts (for example some actual titles alter) and changes in the numbers of books listed all suggest that most of the titles went through several reprints.

The Altemus titles were then taken over for publication in the 1930s by Platt and Munk Co., who reissued most of them, either singly or as composite volumes.

Altemus produced a myriad of different editions of the *Alice* books in all sorts of shapes and sizes, but *Peter Rabbit*, for the most part, survived this type of onslaught, probably because of the success with the standard edition. I do know, however, of at least one edition in a larger format.

Other American firms were not slow to realize the possibilities of pirating *Peter Rabbit*. Charles E. Graham & Co. of New York were soon off the mark with a curious issue where the pictures are grouped together – some before, and some following the actual story – a sure way totally to confuse the child reader.

Whether the Graham Company clearly understood the copyright problem or not is difficult to know, but they exercised a curiously devious ploy when they included *A Fierce Bad Rabbit* and *Miss Moppet* at the end of their edition of *Peter Rabbit*. Such secretive behaviour suggests they knew exactly what they were doing – 'hiding' them away at the back of a 'legitimate piracy'. The ploy was repeated in *Simple Samuel, and Other Stories*, which contains the same two Potter stories – at the end of the book.

The Graham Company were certainly enterprising. Over the next decade they experimented with *Peter Rabbit*, issuing it in a much larger size (26×22.5 cm), but still with Potter's own pictures – though with size and colour changes; an even larger edition (31×26 cm) 'mounted on linen'; and larger still (31.5×26.2 cm) with a new cover illustration by Frances Bowndage.

Trying out different formats was by no means confined to Graham. M. A. Donohue & Co. attempted a huge (38×20.5 cm) 'shaped book' of *Peter Rabbit* in 1913, and employed a new illustrator, C. H. Lawrence. The pictures are still very much Potter influenced, but the break had been made, and it heralded new ventures in illustrative interpretation.

At this stage the Saalfield Publishing Company of Akron, Ohio, come into the picture with the truly astonishing illustrations by Virginia Albert, featuring a ferocious Mrs Rabbit stomping off to market in hobnail boots. The edition must have proved successful as there rapidly followed the wonderfully titled sequels *Peter Rabbit and his Ma* and *Peter Rabbit and his Pa*, written by Louise Field. Potter is left far behind as we find that Flopsy and Mopsy are now male, leaving 'Molly Cottontail' as the single female sibling. Two more books followed – *Peter Rabbit Goes to School* (run by a Miss Peggy Possum) and *Peter Rabbit meets Jimmy Chipmunk.*

In 1972 the maverick firm of Merrimack reissued the first three of these sequels as 'Our version of the antique original', which suggests a certain original success. It perhaps should be added here that this extraordinary firm in the last year or so has also issued a near-facsimile of the genuine Warne edition, complete with a 5-cm toy rabbit.

Beatrix Potter and Warne were slow to publish translations of the Peter Rabbit books, even though work had begun as early as 1907. Their first official version of *Peter Rabbit* (in French) did not appear until 1921. But there were others waiting in the wings. Also in 1921, a pirate French edition was published in New York by Frederick Stokes. They photographed the Warne edition and made plates which are remarkably close to the genuine article. Furthermore it must be said that the Bleriot Johnson translation they employed is much superior to the Warne Ballon/Profichet version.

The Frederick Stokes edition was a solitary beacon of quality. At the other end of the scale was the oddly named *Histoire de Jeannot Lapin* a large, undated paperback version of *Peter Rabbit* with new anonymous illustrations, published by Les Editions Variétes in Montreal (further confusion caused by the title being the same as the Warne French edition of *Benjamin Bunny*). An idea of the joys contained in this book can be gleaned from the first page which gives the siblings' names as: Furet, Gribouille, Adolphe et Jeannot.

The early 1920s also witnessed a quite different set of *Peter Rabbit* sequels – written by Alma Hudson, illustrated by Richard Hudson, and published by the Cupples and Leon Company of New York. There seem to have been at least five titles, starting with *Peter Rabbit and the Fairies.* The books are slightly larger than the Warne/ Altemus mode, the colour pictures are well drawn, with a number of finely detailed line drawings in the text. The quality of the stories is superior to the efforts of the Altemus group, and it is nice to see that Mr Rabbit has returned to life.

By the very nature of the problem, England should have been

free of piracy problems; and such was the case – apart, that is, from one curious episode, when Harrap in 1926 published *The Gingerbread Man* by Sara Cone Bryant. This little book included a story 'When Peter Rabbit had the earache'. Piracy was legitimized at the last moment with a paste-on slip of paper on the last page of the story, giving acknowledgement to Potter at the late legal insistence of both Potter and her publisher.

Back in the USA, the 1930s saw quite a revival of the 'Potter Piracy' business. New illustrators became the norm, though sadly, as is still the case with many books for children, the name of the illustrators were often omitted from the title page. Peter and his family took on all sorts of different appearances – in a Rand McNally 1934 version Mrs Rabbit looked like a hospital matron; by contrast in the slim paperback and 'linenette' versions published by the Sam'l Gabriel Sons Co. of New York, the rabbits were a simple, prettified, Potter-type portrayal.

There were several large paperback editions at about this time. The Whitman company of Racine, Wisconsin, produced a 33×24 cm edition with pictures by Jo Musial, and another featuring Ruth E. Newton's 'Chubby Cubs'. The Merril Publishing Co. of Chicago had a similar-sized interpretation with pictures by the well-known Milo Winter.

Many other artists, known and less well known, attempted *Peter Rabbit*. The Library of Congress lists editions illustrated by John Neill (the illustrator of many *Wizard of Oz* sequels), Nina Jordan, Keith Ward, Florence Nosworthy, Hilda Liloche, Wilma Kane, Phoebe Erickson, Beth Wilson, Theresa Kalab, Anne Scheu Berry, Bill Lohse, Masha and 'Dirk'.

The 1930s also witnessed a renewed interest in 'novelty books', an area dormant since the turn of the century; Potter piracies did not miss out. There was a pop-up version by C. Karey Cloud, a 'moveable' edition by Julian Wehr, and Saalfield of Akron produced *Peter Rabbit with Great Big Cut-outs*. I am sure there were others.

Meanwhile, the Platt and Munk Co., encouraged by the success of their Altemus titles, also issued their own versions of *Peter Rabbit* with the original Potter pictures. These can be found in a number of different guises – hardback and paperback, and in varying sizes.

Walt Disney approached Beatrix Potter in 1936 about making a film of *Peter Rabbit* but she turned him down. At least we have been spared the endless Disney spin-offs that *Alice* has had to endure. For many years the Golden Press organization has produced Disney books for children. Bereft of a Disney film, their version of *Peter Rabbit* (1970) had to make do with pictures by Adriana Mazza Saviozzi.

In more recent years, the issue of 'alternative' editions of *Peter Rabbit* has virtually achieved a status of respectability. All sorts of editions appear in all sorts of styles. In 1946, Theodore Presser Co. of Bryn Mawr, Pennysylvania, published a musical version of *Peter Rabbit*, with music by Ada Richter, a sober, and totally respectable version. Child Guidance Books of New York recently issued a 'Child Guidance Action Book' – a startling book, as the figures move the moment the book is opened because the action of opening operates the mechanism. Saalfield in 1974 issued *Peter Rabbit: a stand-up story book*. No doubt there are many other examples, although in recent years the flow has been stemmed by Warne registering many trademarks to prevent the use of Beatrix Potter's own designs and cover illustrations for unauthorized editions. This has enabled them to stop other publishers claiming legitimacy for their editions.

The most single-minded Potter effort, since the salad days of Altemus, was the series of ten Potter titles issued by Bantam Books in the 1980s, illustrated by Allen Atkinson. He tried his best to get away from the Potter style, in the most part successfully, but with some titles the Potter influence was too much even for him – his Jemima Puddle-duck wears clothes identical to the Potter original. Generally speaking his pictures are a disaster. The books came in for a lot of criticism, to such an extent that I do not think they are now available. Happily the Potter lobby was instrumental in their being withdrawn.

During all this time – since the first publication of *Peter Rabbit* back at the turn of the century – England itself had been free of attempted piracies (apart from the Cone Bryant curiosity mentioned above, and one limp effort – *Peter Rabbit and the Pixies* issued during the 1940s) – until 1987, when a volcano erupted.

Ladybird Books (a sister company of Penguin Books, who own Warne) issued their own *Peter Rabbit* and *Squirrel Nutkin*, illustrated with photographs of specially-constructed models, and with 'simplified text'. These, of course, were not 'piracies' at all, since they were published with the permission of Warne as the copyright owners, but in no way can they be said to be the authentic work of Beatrix Potter, so in my opinion they fall within the general remit of this paper. Protests were loud and vociferous, not least from within the Beatrix Potter Society. Newspaper correspondence columns rang with indignation. Opinion from the general public was sharply divided between those who were outraged and those who took a more practical view and saw the books as an early introduction to the originals for children who were learning to read for themselves and who would find the originals difficult to manage. But the furore showed how strongly people feel about the original editions. Sadly the first two titles have been joined by *Jemima Puddle-Duck* and *The Tale of Two Bad Mice*. Let us hope that the calendars and collectibles will not follow.

As I write, we are approaching the end of the official copyright period, due in 1994, fifty years from the death of Beatrix Potter. In 1987 Warne published reoriginated books, for which new plates were made from the original artwork, in volumes clearly marked 'The Original and Authorized Edition'. The books are resplendent in all their original detail, and colour. They should be enough; certainly the experience of the USA would indicate so, where despite the amazingly diverse editions of the *Peter Rabbit* books over the years people overwhelmingly prefer the original ones. The 'pirates' have never lasted long.

'Excessively Impertinent Bunnies' began as a lecture given in Oxford in early May 1988 as part of the Opie Appeal to raise money for securing the Opie Collection of Children's Literature for the Bodleian Library. Later that month Humphrey Carpenter adapted his talk for the Seventh Annual Linder Memorial Lecture of the Beatrix Potter Society in London, when his title was 'The Jane Austen of the Nursery: Beatrix Potter as Stylist'. The full version of 'Excessively Impertinent Bunnies' can be found in Children and Their Books *(O.U.P., 1989).*

EXCESSIVELY IMPERTINENT BUNNIES: THE SUBVERSIVE ELEMENT IN BEATRIX POTTER

HUMPHREY CARPENTER, 1989

> They are holed up in some bar among the dives
> of Deptford, deep in their cups, and a packet
> of cashew nuts, like Chippy Hackee and cute
> little Timmy Tiptoes hiding from their wives.

THIS VERSE FROM the sonnet by Blake Morrison was printed in *The Times Literary Supplement* in April 1987. Beatrix Potter enthusiasts will not need to have it explained that Morrison is comparing the couple of blokes he has seen in the Deptford pub with Potter's *The Tale of Timmy Tiptoes*, in which a squirrel and a

chipmunk hide away from their wives at the bottom of a hollow tree and stuff themselves full of nuts.

It is a bit of a jolt to find Beatrix Potter cited in such a context. We would not have been surprised if it had been *Alice in Wonderland*, for Lewis Carroll is ceaselessly plundered, to the point of cliché, by writers, poets, and speech-makers. Carroll is respectable as a literary influence; T.S. Eliot lectured on him on at least one occasion, and you can detect Carrollian influences in his poetry. But it is hard to imagine the late Dame Helen Gardner citing *The Tale of Peter Rabbit* in her *Art of T.S. Eliot*. Chroniclers of the development of the twentieth-century literary imagination are not likely to put Beatrix Potter on the map as a source for poets and novelists. Yet one modern novelist writes:

> Of course there was Beatrix Potter. I have never lost my admiration for her books and I have often reread her, so that I am not surprised when I find in one of my own stories, 'Under the Garden', a pale echo of Tom Kitten being trounced up [*sic*] by the rats behind the skirting-board and the sinister Anna Maria covering him with dough, and in *Brighton Rock* the dishonest lawyer . . . hungrily echoes Miss Potter's dialogue as he watches the secretaries go by carrying their little typewriters.

This passage is taken from Graham Greene's autobiography. The short story he refers to, 'Under the Garden', is not just a 'pale echo' of the Beatrix Potter *Tale of Samuel Whiskers*; it is an elaborate commentary on it, and I shall come back to it later. As to the *Brighton Rock* passage, here it is:

> 'I married beneath me,' Mr Prewitt said. 'It was my tragic mistake. I was young. An affair of uncontrollable passion. I was a passionate man,' he said, wriggling with indigestion . . . He leant forward and said in a whisper – 'I watch the little typists go by carrying their little cases. I'm quite harmless. A man may watch. My God, how neat and trim.' He broke off, his hand vibrating on the chair arm.

The source of this is *The Tale of Ginger and Pickles*, the Potter book about the dog and cat who keep the village shop:

> The shop was also patronized by mice – only the mice were rather afraid of Ginger [the cat].
> Ginger usually requested Pickles to serve them, because he said it made his mouth water.
> 'I cannot bear,' said he, 'to see them going out at the door carrying their little parcels.'
> 'I have the same feeling about rats,' replied Pickles, 'but it would never do to eat our own customers; they would leave us and go to Tabitha Twitchit's.'
> 'On the contrary, they would go nowhere,' replied Ginger gloomily.

Greene's revelation of his debt to Beatrix Potter, his statement that he has 'often reread her', sent me hunting in the indexes of some other twentieth-century literary autobiographies and biographies. The catch was only so-so. W.H. Auden admitted to a lifelong fondness for her books; he writes in 'Letter to Lord Byron':

> You must ask me who
> Have written just as I'd have liked to do.
> I stop to listen and the names I hear
> Are those of Firbank, Potter, Carroll, Lear.

Similarly Christopher Isherwood's biographer tells us that *The Tale of Samuel Whiskers* was 'one of the first books to have left its mark' on Isherwood in childhood, and points out that the more macabre elements in the Potter stories evidently contributed to the lurid 'Mortmere' fantasies which Isherwood and his friend Edward Upward concocted during undergraduate days – fantasies which themselves influenced the writings of the entire 'Auden generation'.

But such acknowledgements of the importance of the Potter stories on writers' imaginations in childhood are rare. If Evelyn Waugh or Virginia Woolf, Robert Graves or Stephen Spender ever read, cared for, and were affected by Potter, they or their biographers do not bother to tell us. (George Orwell's biographer Bernard Crick records that Orwell was still reading Potter, particularly *The Tale of Pigling Bland*, when he was at preparatory school and, as Orwell's sister said, 'far too old for it'; but tantalizingly Crick fails to make the obvious link with *Animal Farm*.) Beatrix Potter gets no mention at all in a 1981 encyclopaedia entitled *Makers of Modern Culture*, and though she appears briefly in the 1983 *Fontana Biographical Companion to Modern Thought*, the entry for her there scarcely explains her importance to, say, Auden or Graham Greene. We are told that she wrote 'illustrated tales about rabbits, kittens, mice and other creatures', and that these were within the 'well-established tradition' of 'the anthropomorphic animal story, often with moral attitudes'. Her originality 'was in the quality of her illustrations, drawn from life, and their aptness to the text. Rarely portraying humans, she captured essentially animal characteristics and, latterly, a feeling of the Lakeland landscape. Word and picture were used in an absolutely complementary sense.'

Now it is perfectly true that everyone who has opened a Beatrix Potter book remembers her pictures. Anthony Powell, another novelist of the Graham Greene generation, refers in his autobiography to the feeling that Aubrey Beardsley's drawings were 'familiar as Tenniel's Alice or Beatrix Potter's Tom Kitten'. But it is not for this, not for drawings of Tom Kitten or the Lake District, that Greene, Auden, Isherwood, and Blake Morrison have admired

and been affected by her. Greene has 're*read*' her; Auden wished to
have written, not drawn, like her; Isherwood acquired from her
books not an interest in 'tales about rabbits, kittens, mice and other
creatures', nor the 'moral attitudes' of the long-established anthropomorphic animal story, but – judging from Mortmere – a sense of
the way that the grotesque and unmentionable may lurk behind any
domestic façade, particularly the most respectable.

This is precisely the use Graham Greene makes of her in the short
story he modestly calls 'a pale echo' of *The Tale of Samuel Whiskers*.
'Under the Garden', first collected in Greene's *A Sense of Reality*,
describes Wilditch, an elderly man dying of cancer, returning to the
country house where he was brought up. He has come for one
purpose: to see if there could possibly be any truth in a vivid
memory he has of one night in childhood when, wishing to hide
from his family, he penetrated to the mysterious inner reaches of the
garden, crossed a lake to an island, discovered a passage leading
underground between the roots of a tree, and descended to a dark
and sinister region. At that moment he hears a hoarse voice calling
'Maria, Maria', whereupon:

> An old woman appeared suddenly and noiselessly around the
> corner of the passage. She wore an old blue dress which came
> down to her ankles . . . She was every bit as surprised as I was.
> She stood there gaping at me and then she opened her mouth and
> squawked. I learned later that she had no roof to her mouth and
> was probably saying, 'Who are you?' . . . The hoarse voice out of
> sight said, 'Bring him along here, Maria.'

We would not need Greene's own admission to identify the story's
model. Even the woman's name comes from Beatrix Potter:

> When Tom Kitten picked himself up and looked about him –
> he found himself in a place that he had never seen before,
> although he had lived all his life in the house . . .

Opposite to him – as far away as he could sit – was an enormous rat . . .

'Anna Maria! Anna Maria!' squeaked the rat. There was a pattering noise and an old woman rat poked her head round a rafter.

All in a minute she rushed upon Tom Kitten . . .

In Beatrix Potter's illustration, as in Greene's story, Anna Maria wears a long blue dress that comes down to her ankles.

In Greene's version, Samuel Whiskers, the old rat of the Potter story, becomes an ancient man permanently seated on a lavatory, 'a big old man with a white beard . . . He had one good leg, but the right trouser was sewn up and looked stuffed like a bolster.' This figure of nightmare tells the boy to call him Javitt – though mentioning that this is not his real name – and makes it clear that the boy will be kept prisoner, so as to read aloud to him from a bundle of ancient newspapers; a detail recalling Tony Last's imprisonment by Mr Todd in Evelyn Waugh's *A Handful of Dust* – which incidentally leads us back to Beatrix Potter, for 'Mr Tod' is the name of one of her own principal characters in her most sinister story. (Todd and Tod both occupy sinister houses in the middle of the woodland, remote from human society.) . . .

'Under the Garden' does not quite come off as a story. . . . The qualities of Beatrix Potter elude Greene, and Javitt lacks most of the resonance she achieved in her usual terse manner when she created Samuel Whiskers. But one values the story for Greene's tribute to the force of her imagination, the acknowledgement that she had the power of creating archetypes that remain with her readers for the rest of their lives. And if one wants an indication that the Potter influence can fit snugly into modern writing, one need only turn back the pages to the very first piece in Greene's *Collected Short Stories*. 'The Destructors', dated 1954 and anticipating the vandalism of a later generation, describes a group of teenagers breaking into an old man's house while he is away one Bank Holiday – an exceptionally fine house with a unique carved staircase – and destroying not merely the contents but the structure itself, in an orgy of pointless waste. Again there is a strong echo of Potter:

> Then Tom Thumb lost his temper. He put the ham in the middle of the floor, and hit it with the tongs and with the shovel – bang, bang, smash, smash!
>
> The ham flew all into pieces, for underneath the shiny paint it was made of nothing but plaster!
>
> Then there was no end to the rage and disappointment of Tom Thumb and Hunca Munca. They broke up the pudding, the lobsters, the pears and oranges . . .
>
> [Tom Thumb] took Jane's clothes out of the chest of drawers in her bedroom, and he threw them out of the top floor window.

This is from *The Tale of Two Bad Mice*, in which the mice systematically destroy and plunder the contents of a doll's house.

No doubt an indefatigable researcher could find traces of Potter elsewhere in Graham Greene's work; after all, the structure of his early novels, which usually deal with a man on the run who is saved by a girl he has met in his flight, bears a distinct resemblance to *The Tale of Pigling Bland.*

Greene's Beatrix Potter, then, is not the Lakeland watercolourist who was solely concerned with 'essentially animal characteristics'. That definition of Potter would appear to be very wide of the mark. In fact anyone with a more than superficial acquaintance with the Potter books knows it to be upside down. Like any other animal fabulist from Aesop onwards, she invariably uses the creatures in her stories to display human characteristics and foibles. She can heighten and underline their character-traits because she is not obliged to clutter her stories with unnecessary social background, and she can also eliminate such elements as sexuality, so as to concentrate her attention on her themes. There is no need to waste space demonstrating this: anyone who troubles to read her stories with the slightest attention can see it. The question is: what is exclusively Potterish about the way she does it? Why should it be her animal stories, rather than Aesop's or Joel Chandler Harris's or Alison Uttley's, that stuck in the imaginations of Greene, Auden, Isherwood, and maybe George Orwell too?

If we look again at what that Fontana encyclopaedia has to say about Beatrix Potter's texts, we find that she wrote in 'a well-established tradition' of 'the anthropomorphic animal story, often with moral attitudes'. Such a tradition certainly existed, though Aesop was not part of it – his animals are pragmatic, and his tales demonstrate the virtues of common sense and looking after one's own skin, rather than offering any more lofty moral fare. Nor are 'moral attitudes' found in the work of Joel Chandler Harris, the most accomplished practitioner of the animal fable for children before Potter's time. Harris's *Uncle Remus* is a hymn to cunning and ingenious trickery, and it preaches a frontier survival-ethic rather than nineteenth-century Christian morality.. . . Her line does go back to Aesop, and it takes in something of *Uncle Remus* on the way

– it was one of her own favourite books in childhood. But there is nothing in her work that resembles the moral tale. In fact it might be argued that she is writing something pretty close to a series of immoral tales; that the voice we hear again and again in her stories is not that of the late Victorian spinster decorously instructing her nieces and child-friends in acceptable social behaviour, but of a rebel, albeit a covert one, demonstrating the rewards of nonconformity, and exhorting her young readers to question the social system into which they found themselves born. . . .

The 'voice' in the Beatrix Potter books would seem, at first encounter, to be a Victorian one. If you ask people what they chiefly remember about the stories, apart from the pictures, the answer is likely to be 'the long words'. She is famous, perhaps even infamous, for the demands she makes on child readers. 'I am affronted,' says Mrs Tabitha Twitchit when she finds that her kittens have made a mess of their clothes; and we are told in the same story that the

kittens' behaviour 'disturbed the dignity and repose of the tea party'. Jemima Puddle-Duck, much put out because her eggs are taken from her and given to a hen to hatch, 'complained of the superfluous hen'. Tommy Brock in *The Tale of Mr. Tod* 'squeezed himself into the rabbit hole with alacrity'. In the same story, one of the rabbits complains: 'My Uncle Bouncer has displayed a lamentable want of discretion for his years'; and words like 'indolent' and 'apoplectic' are used to portray the behaviour of Tommy Brock the badger, snoring as he lies in bed in his boots. It seems to be an orgy of Victorian vocabulary. The present-day parent, attempting to explain these words to children vaguely supposes that the original readers, in the first decade of this century, when the books were appearing, could take it all in their stride.

But could they? The years between *The Tale of Peter Rabbit* and *The Tale of Pigling Bland*, the first and last notable Potter stories, were 1901 to 1913, years in which Kenneth Grahame, J.M. Barrie, and E. Nesbit were writing for children in a variety of thoroughly un-Victorian styles; years when, to look at the wider world, Joyce, Eliot, and Pound were beginning their modernist experiments. Other picture-books for small children dating from the early 1900s, such as L. Leslie Brooke's *Johnny Crow's Garden* or Florence Upton's 'Golliwogg' series, are quite without the Victorianisms of the Potter books. What is going on? Was Beatrix Potter a stranded survivor of the Victorian age, unable to jettison the diction of her parents' world, or was she consciously imitating the manners of an earlier age, and if so, why?

If you look at them carefully, her so-called Victorianisms reveal themselves as not Victorian at all. Victorians did not write that way, certainly not for children and usually not for adults. Victorian English tends to be very wordy; the Potter archaisms, or what we might call antiquities of style, are strikingly crisp. They say in one word – 'affronted', 'discretion', 'alacrity' – what a true Victorian would have rambled over several sentences to convey. Consider this:

> It was almost too much happiness to bear. Oliver felt stunned and stupefied by the unexpected intelligence; he could not weep, or speak, or rest. He had scarcely the power of understanding anything that had passed, until, after a long ramble in the quiet evening air, a burst of tears came to his relief, and he seemed to awaken, all at once, to a full sense of the joyful change that had occurred, and the almost insupportable load of anguish which had been taken from his breast.

This passage was chosen virtually at random from *Oliver Twist*. Compare Beatrix Potter describing the return home of an entire family of young children who have nearly been cooked and eaten alive:

> Great was old Mr. Bouncer's relief and Flopsy's joy when Peter and Benjamin arrived in triumph with the young family. The rabbit-babies were rather tumbled and very hungry; they were fed and put to bed. They soon recovered.

If Beatrix Potter, writing this in 1912, is looking back stylistically, her glance seems to have travelled beyond the Victorian age, back to an earlier period when written English was an instrument capable of greater precision.

You can see why she was doing this if you look at her journal. One of the few regular diversions that family life offered when she was young was conversation with her paternal grandmother. Old Mrs Potter, née Jessie Crompton, had been born in 1801, if not quite 'In the time of swords and periwigs and full-skirted coats with flowered lappets', as Beatrix Potter has it in the opening paragraph of *The Tailor of Gloucester*, then certainly into a society that seemed as remote from late-Victorian London as Beatrix Potter's own times seem from ours. Margaret Lane tells us how, in early childhood, Beatrix would delight to hide under the table in her grandmother's house and eavesdrop on the old lady's talk. Later, she made a methodical business of writing it down in her journal, like a modern researcher collecting oral history of a bygone age. Here she is at the age of twenty-one recording a 'scene, at lunch':

> My grandmother disapproved, in a state of high and violent indignation and dispute with the rest of the family, as to the cautious pace at which the coachman drives the mares . . . 'Eh – dear – *I* k-now, – I've been, in, gigs, with – my fa-ther – why – we were – *all*, thrown, out, of, – a – gig – at once (roars of laughter) . . .

And three years earlier, again in the journal, she describes the old lady's appearance:

> How pretty she does look with her grey curls, under her muslin cap, trimmed with black lace. Her plain crêpe dress with broad grey linen collar and cuffs turned over. So erect and always on the move, with her gentle face and waken [*sic*], twinkling eyes. There is no one like grandmamma. She always seems to me as near perfect as is possible here . . .

Perfection is identified with the Regency period in which her grandmother had been brought up; note how Beatrix imitates the diction of that age in the journal entries: 'a state of high and violent indignation', 'waken, twinkling eyes'. As to the costume she describes, in old age Beatrix herself adopted it – the same muslin cap can be seen in many late pictures of her – and she seemingly modelled her behaviour on her grandmother. One also notes that it was very soon after her grandmother's death that she began, in 1893, to write the picture-letters to children of her acquaintance which provided the first material for her books. They were an act of recreating her grandmother's world.

The Beatrix Potter character most resembling her grandmother is Mrs Tiggy-winkle, the hedgehog washerwoman, who wears the muslin cap and has the twinkling eyes of old Mrs Potter. But the old lady's influence on the books goes much deeper. The second book that Beatrix wrote, immediately after she had begun to make a name for herself with *The Tale of Peter Rabbit* was *The Tailor of Gloucester*, first published in 1902. This is the story which Beatrix herself preferred above all the others she wrote, which may seem odd, for it bears remarkably little resemblance in

theme and style to the rest of her work. She liked it so much (one guesses) because it is an exercise in recreating the speech-rhythms of her grandmother's era, the age into which Beatrix herself evidently wished she had been born:

> He cut his coats without waste, according to his embroidered cloth; they were very small ends and snippets that lay about upon the table – 'Too narrow breadths for nought – except waistcoats for mice,' said the tailor. . . .
> 'No breadth at all, and cut on the cross; it is no breadth at all; tippets for mice and ribbons for mobs! for mice!' said the Tailor of Gloucester.

Now, these are in fact not the rhythms of late eighteenth- and early nineteenth-century English prose; not at all. As so often when a writer sets out to recapture the style of an earlier period, what results is something quite new. One can detect all sorts of influences on *The Tailor of Gloucester*. There is a hint of Anglo-Saxon poetry in the alliteration ('He cut his coats without waste, according to his embroidered cloth'), and at times the book seems to be almost an operatic libretto: an aria by the Tailor is interrupted by a chattering chorus of mice, and the central section is made up of a sequence of Christmas rhymes, chanted by birds and beasts 'from all the roofs and gables and old wooden houses in Gloucester'. Possibly one hears an echo of Browning – the story is a kind of *Pied Piper* in reverse, set amid the alleyways of an ancient city, with the Tailor freeing the mice from imprisonment and threatened extinction. But the voice that comes through most strongly is that of the Authorized Version of the Bible.

The reiterated 'said the tailor . . . said the Tailor of Gloucester' echoes 'saith the Lord . . . saith the Lord God' so often found in the writings of the prophets, while the characteristic Beatrix Potter sentence, which first appears fully-fledged in *The Tailor of Gloucester*, is composed of two balanced halves divided by a caesura, in the manner of the Psalms. And like the psalmist, Potter often uses the second half to introduce a disarming qualification, or some nuance:

> All that day he was ill, and the next day, and the next; and what should become of the cherry-coloured coat?

> Out of doors the market folks went trudging through the snow to buy their geese and turkeys, and to bake their Christmas pies; but there would be no Christmas dinner for Simpkin and the poor old Tailor of Gloucester.

With which compare:

> For the Lord knoweth the way of the righteous; but the way of the ungodly shall perish. (Psalm 1)

– or indeed hundreds of other verses in the psalms. Beatrix Potter herself spoke of 'The sweet rhythm of the authorized translation', and one notes that she says 'rhythm' rather than 'language': it is the rise and fall, the biblical cadence, that she picks up and uses in her later books to fine ironical effect. For example: 'He snored peacefully and regularly; but one eye was not perfectly shut.'

The Tailor of Gloucester is not ironical. It is an idyllic recreation of her grandmother's age, and also, in its miniaturist way, a piece of social commentary that might have been dreamt up by Ruskin or William Morris. It evokes a pre-industrial arcadia, a perfect city where the skill of the individual craftsman plays a vital part in the social system: the Tailor is making a wedding coat for the Mayor of Gloucester, who is to be married on Christmas morning, and the wedding cannot take place without the coat. The central device of the story, the mice stepping in to finish the job when the Tailor is taken ill, is a reworking of a well-known fairy-story motif, found (for example) in the Grimms' fairy tale 'The Elves and the Shoemaker'; but Potter gives it a nice sharp social edge, for her story, though set in an ultra-hierarchical society, reverses the usual order of power. Instead of the Mayor and the rich men of the city controlling events, the Mayor is beholden to the poor Tailor, the Tailor depends upon his cat Simpkin, whom he needs to go out and buy the missing skein of cherry-coloured silk, and in the end everyone's fate hangs on the skill and good nature of the mice, the

very lowest creatures of all in the city's pecking order. *The Tailor of Gloucester* thus presents a society that is in every way an opposite to the imperfections and injustices of urban industrial life in the early 1900s, when it was written.

Its companion piece, written and published three years later, is *The Tale of Mrs. Tiggy-Winkle*, again arcadian and idyllic in character, again intended to portray a perfect society in which the lowest person in the hierarchy – in this case a washerwoman – is able to pull the controlling strings. Mrs Tiggy-winkle, though constantly giving reminders of her low position in the class system – 'Oh, yes, if you please'm . . . Oh no, if you please'm' – is really a person of great influence, since she supplies clean clothes to all the animals – and clothes, as we shall see, are for Potter's characters the visible sign of their identity and individuality. She even has some influence over the lives of humans. The child Lucie comes all the way up the mountainside in search of her own missing handkerchiefs, which Mrs Tiggy-winkle has indeed washed and ironed. But the book is one of Potter's less secure inventions. Lucie is an uncomfortable intrusion from the real world, and the animals' clothes, such as Peter Rabbit's blue jacket, become confused with their skins – Mrs Tiggy-winkle's wash includes 'woolly coats belonging to the little lambs' and a 'velvety black moleskin waist-coat'. Quite apart from the whimsy, Potter seems to have lost her grip on her own scheme. Her unease is betrayed by the uncertain narrative tone throughout the book ('Lucie opened the door: and what do you think there was inside the hill?'; a questioning, condescending manner that she never uses elsewhere) and by the fact that at the end it is suggested that the entire story may have been a dream.

The Tailor of Gloucester, then, could not be successfully imitated, not even by its own author. *Mrs. Tiggy-Winkle* is by Beatrix Potter's standards a narrative failure, memorable verbally only for its depiction of the stone-flagged kitchen, 'a nice clean kitchen with a flagged floor and wooden beams . . . just like any other farm kitchen'. . . . But *The Tailor of Gloucester* itself was a crucially important book for Potter, a linguistic exercise, a study in establishing what she believed to be her grandmother's voice. Once she had practised this successfully, she could use that voice in a wide range of narrative contexts.

The theme she had chosen to tackle in her earliest story, *The Tale of Peter Rabbit*, is one that recurs throughout her work, until it comes to final resolution in *The Tale of Pigling Bland*: Jack in the Giant's castle, the little fellow, the folk-tale hero who has nothing but his courage and his wits, struggling against an opponent of far superior physical strength. That she should choose such a theme is not very surprising – it predominates in Grimms' fairy tales and many of the other classic folk-tale collections, and it was perhaps a natural subject for someone congenitally shy, who viewed the prospect of any encounter with a stranger with considerable anxiety. It is perhaps too fanciful to suppose that the oppressors in her stories – Mr McGregor, Old Brown the owl in *Squirrel Nutkin*, Samuel Whiskers, and the others – unconsciously stood in her mind for her own parents? It was in their home that she was trapped for much of her life, like Peter Rabbit caught by the buttons of his own jacket; and certainly the flight of Pigling Bland and Pig-wig from Mr Thomas Piperson in her 1913 book seems to refer to her own final escape that very year from the family fold – 1913 was when she married William Heelis and at last became independent, at the age of forty-seven.

The subject, then, is not surprising. The moral attitude of the narrator in these stories is. Far from following the 'well-established tradition' of English children's stories about animals, and exhorting the reader to good and docile behaviour, the narrator of *Peter Rabbit* and its successors is definitely on the side of the transgressors. After all, Peter is a burglar, breaking into Mr McGregor's garden to steal vegetables. More than that, he is a familiar figure from the Victorian moral tale, the disobedient child. His mother has specifically forbidden him to go into the garden, for the very good reason that 'your Father had an accident there; he was put in a pie by Mrs McGregor'. (Note the un-Victorian understatement of 'accident'.) Peter's sisters are 'good little bunnies' and they dutifully go down the lane to gather blackberries; at the end they are rewarded with 'bread and milk and blackberries for supper', while Peter is 'not very well' after his escapade and is dosed with 'camomile tea'. So far, everything is conventional: the disobedient boy meets his deserts. And yet – 'good little bunnies' – isn't there a touch of sarcasm here?

Certainly Peter has lost his 'blue jacket with brass buttons, quite new', but he has daringly got into the giant's lair, has rewarded himself with the treasure ('First he ate some lettuces and some French beans; and then he ate some radishes'); and he has escaped through his own exertions – something of which the 'good little bunnies' would be quite incapable. Strikingly, in this first of the Beatrix Potter books, the only antiquity of diction appears at the moment of crisis:

> Peter gave himself up for lost, and shed big tears; but his sobs were overheard by some friendly sparrows, who flew to him in great excitement, and implored him to exert himself.

'Implored him to exert himself' is the language of the eighteenth-century moral tales which Grandmother Potter would have read in her own childhood; indeed Beatrix herself had found it in the stories of Maria Edgeworth, which she had been given to read in the nursery. People in the Edgeworth stories and the old moral tales are always being exhorted to exert themselves, to shake off slovenly ways, to raise themselves in society by their own exertions. And here we have a rabbit struggling to exert himself to get out of a gooseberry net. It is surely a parody, a gentle mockery of the old-style children's story. The leg of the moral tale is being gently but quite definitely pulled.

Next comes *The Tailor of Gloucester*, and then in 1903 we are back with the little fellow in the giant's lair, this time Squirrel Nutkin taunting Old Brown the owl with his mocking riddles and only just escaping with his life, minus not just a jacket but a tail. Again, Nutkin is the transgressor – he deliberately infuriates the august personage on whose land the squirrels are gathering nuts; the rest of

them, like the 'good little bunnies', are respectful to their elders and speak politely to Old Brown ('Old Mr Brown, will you favour us with your permission . . .?'), but Nutkin, we are told, 'was excessively impertinent in his manners' – an observation straight from the moral tale. And, as in *Peter Rabbit*, the narrator is undoubtedly on Nutkin's side. Nutkin may nearly come to grief, but he has certainly (in Eliot's words) dared disturb the universe, has challenged the accepted order. And he has done it, one notes, by reviving a very ancient form of taunting, the riddle-game, which belongs to a more robust age than that which spawned the moral tale. Beatrix Potter does not necessarily intend that her young readers should emulate Nutkin, but she undoubtedly prefers his spirit and enterprise to the dull conformity of the well-behaved squirrels, and this is why, when she describes his *hubris*, she does so in a voice that mocks those who disapprove of it. He is just the sort of character whom the old writers of the moral tale would have called 'excessively impertinent'. Well, she seems to be saying, good for him.

So she is evoking her grandmother's world not entirely in admiration. The grandmother herself was admired by Beatrix for her spirited diction and independence of mind – a vigorous contrast to the caution and nervousness of Beatrix's parents – but Beatrix recognized that the world in which the old lady had grown up was alarmingly repressive towards children. Or perhaps she is simply recalling her own childhood reading, for the attitudes of the moral tale persisted in children's books, up to and even beyond the late nineteenth-century revolution inaugurated by Lewis Carroll, and Beatrix would certainly have been soaked in them from her own nursery reading. Like Lewis Carroll's Alice, the narrator of *Peter Rabbit* and its successors is striking a blow for independence and a freer moral attitude towards children. The Potter mockery of the moral tale parallels Lewis Carroll's mockery of the sanctimonious religious verses of Isaac Watts in the Alice books.

This satirical element slackens off a little in the next story in the Peter Rabbit sequence. *The Tale of Benjamin Bunny* is mainly an exercise in narrative understatement. Its subject is Peter's paralysing fear on his return to the garden to rescue his jacket, and, like a Hemingway novel, the narrative constantly sidesteps specifying the emotion that is being experienced: 'They got amongst flower-pots, and frames and tubs; Peter heard noises worse than ever, his eyes were as big as lolly-pops!' (Notice the 'got' in the first half of this sentence – not 'correct writing', then or now, but frequently used by Potter to achieve another sort of biblical echo: 'The sun got round behind the wood, and it was quite late in the afternoon; but still the cat sat upon the basket.' So 'they got amongst thieves' in the

Bible.) Another feature of *Benjamin Bunny* is the use of the pictures not just, as that encyclopaedia entry said, in an 'absolutely complementary sense', but actually to say more than the text. The narrator merely states that old Mr Bunny, having rescued his son and nephew from Mr McGregor's garden, 'took out his nephew Peter', but the picture shows him whipping Peter soundly for his disobedience.

The Tale of Two Bad Mice is purely satirical. It mocks the mores of a consumer society where the rich live amid entirely useless objects. Into a doll's house come two mice, Tom Thumb and Hunca Munca, whose names – from Fielding's satirical *Tom Thumb* play – announce disruptive farce. They find that the food set out on the dining table is 'extremely beautiful', but 'it would not come off the plates', so in baffled rage they set about destruction and looting. Again it is quite clear where the narrator's sympathies lie: not with the blandly smiling, richly dressed, entirely inanimate dolls – 'Jane was the Cook; but she never did any cooking, because the dinner had been bought ready-made, in a box full of shavings . . . Jane leant against the kitchen dresser and smiled – but neither of them made any remark.' Like the food, they are beautiful and fake. No, the narrator is on the side of the live mice, who unlike most of Potter's animal protagonists are unclothed, as if to emphasize their very real animal energy. Tom Thumb's destruction of the plaster-of-Paris ham and all the other fake food goes without authorial reproof, and though there is a token gesture of repentance towards the end of the story – the mice 'pay' for what they have broken and stolen with a crooked sixpence, and Hunca Munca becomes the dolls' charlady – the mice's 'badness' earns no more disapproval from Potter than does the cheek of Squirrel Nutkin or the daring of Peter Rabbit.

Having virtually advocated social revolution in *Two Bad Mice*, Beatrix Potter next shows, in *The Pie and The Patty-Pan*, the absurd consequences of taking too seriously the niceties of upper-middle-class social behaviour. *Two Bad Mice* portrays elegant English society viewed from outside; *The Pie and The Patty-Pan* shows it

from within, where it looks even sillier. Two elegant personages –
Ribby and Duchess, a cat and a dog – arrange to have an elegant
tea-party together. One of them is too well brought up to tell the
other of her dietary preferences, with absurd comic consequences.
These are two village spinsters tangling themselves in their own
etiquette. At the height of the comedy, the victim's chief emotion is
social embarrassment:

> It was most conspicuous. All the village could see that Ribby
> was fetching the doctor.
> 'I *knew* they would over-eat themselves!' said Cousin Tabitha
> Twitchit.

The doctor is portrayed as a social inferior – as doctors were
regarded in the days of Beatrix Potter's childhood. Dr Maggoty, a
large magpie, has a strikingly vulgar turn of speech ('"Gammon?
ha! HA!" said he, with his head on one side'), and he offers a very
coarse remedy for Duchess supposedly having swallowed the
patty-pan – a bread pill. It appears, indeed, that the whole tea party,
elegant as the participants have tried to make it, has transgressed the
social code:

Cousin Tabitha was disdainful afterwards in conversation –
'A little *dog* indeed! Just as if there were no CATS in Sawrey!
And a *pie* for afternoon tea! The very idea!' said Cousin Tabitha
Twitchit.

Again, note the antiquated terminology. Sawrey, the scene of *The
Pie and The Patty-Pan*, has become another Cranford. The story is
only superficially set in Near Sawrey, Beatrix Potter's Lake District
village, which is just a tiny hamlet. The society she is really
mocking is the genteel world of Kensington. Incidentally Hill Top,
the farmhouse she bought in Near Sawrey, was altered by her in a
fashion that largely evokes the Kensington of her childhood: she
installed an ornate fireplace in the ground floor inner parlour, and
upstairs built an elegant drawing-room to house her brother
Bertram's enormous landscape paintings.

The theme of the little fellow in the giant's castle is resumed in
The Tale of Mr. Jeremy Fisher, one of the first stories Beatrix Potter
had written, though it was not published until 1906. This time the
victim is not merely preyed upon by bigger creatures – an enormous trout swallows Jeremy Fisher but spits him out again because
it dislikes the taste of his mackintosh,
surely a prankish reference to the exploits
of Jonah – but is himself a predator.
Jeremy Fisher digs up worms for bait,
catches minnows, and dines on 'roasted
grasshopper with lady-bird sauce'. The
simple Jack-and-the-Giant motif has
widened into a realistic portrayal of an
aggressive natural world. After his
encounter with the trout, Mr Jeremy loses
some of his clothes and consequently
most of his dignity – 'he hopped home

across the meadow with his mackintosh all in tatters' – but by the
end he has resumed his pretensions, donning (as the illustration
shows us) a Regency waistcoat and tail-coat, breeches, spats, and

pointed shoes to welcome his friends to an elegant meal. The story highlights the absurd contrast between the rough and tumble of real life and the pretensions of society.

That theme is more explicitly worked out in *The Tale of Tom Kitten*, in which the social pretensions of Mrs Tabitha Twitchit – always in the Potter books a paragon, as her name might suggest, of  nervously correct behaviour – come to naught when she tries to dress her kittens for a smart tea-party. Clothes are again used as symbols of social pretension – 'all sorts of elegant uncomfortable clothes' the narrator calls them; whereas the kittens 'had dear little fur coats of their own; and they tumbled about the doorstep and played in the dust'. This state of nature is not suitable for the 'fine company' Mrs Twitchit has invited to call, so she forces the kittens into pinafores, bibs, and tuckers. These quickly fall off, and are put on in jest by those very farmyard creatures whom their mother has particularly warned the kittens against, as social untouchables – the Puddle-ducks. 'I am affronted,' says Mrs Twitchit when she contemplates her children's behaviour, and once again the stilted language separates Beatrix Potter herself from the sentiment. Nor does she approve of Mrs Twitchit telling a lie to keep up appearances:

> She sent them upstairs; and I am sorry to say she told her friends that they were in bed with the measles; which was not true.
>
> Quite the contrary; they were not in bed: *not* in the least.
>
> Somehow there were very extraordinary noises over-head, which disturbed the dignity and repose of the tea party.

From the comic clothing of the Puddle-ducks in the kittens' pretentious garments it is an easy step to *The Tale of Jemima Puddle-Duck*, a masterly reworking of the Red Riding Hood theme, in which Jemima's folly is emphasized by her donning of clothes – 'a shawl and a poke bonnet' – as she unwisely abandons the security of the farmyard (an extended family in which everyone helps each other) and attempts hubristically to hatch her eggs in seclusion. At the end, after the disastrous failure of her venture, she is back again in her natural unclothed state. A striking thing is Potter's own obvious contempt for the naïve Jemima, who surrenders herself trustingly into the hands of 'the gentleman with sandy whiskers', a fox whose manner and costume suggest the caddish seducer of a dairymaid, a veritable Alec D'Urberville. Jemima is a poor foolish thing in comparison with his elegant diction and behaviour. Similarly in *The Tale of Samuel Whiskers*, originally published in 1908 as *The Roly-Poly Pudding*,

Potter's sympathies are clearly with the ingenious, unscrupulous rats rather than with the hapless Tom Kitten; though Tom's enterprise in climbing up the chimney to escape imprisonment on baking day is clearly to be preferred to his sisters' caution, to his restraining, socially-conscious mother (Tabitha Twitchit again), and to her censorious neighbour Mrs Ribby (the cat from *The Pie and The Patty-Pan*).

The Roly-Poly Pudding, to give it the original and more appropriate title, is Potter's most resonant and multi-layered story. No wonder Graham Greene wanted to explore its implications. We may see Freudian symbolism in Tom's search up the sooty chimney of his mother's house; but if his journey away from the maternal clutches has something about it of sexual exploration, the rats themselves, omnivorous, cantankerous, and lurking under the very floorboards of an ordinary room, seem to be symbols far older than Freud and his discoveries – almost Homeric in their power over the imagination. And it is to them that Potter gives her most consistently antiquarian language. They speak in the tones of the moral tale, to richly comic effect, for they are, of course, pure amorality:

'Will not the string be very indigestible, Anna Maria?' inquired Samuel Whiskers.

Anna Maria said she thought that it was of no consequence; but she wished that Tom Kitten would hold his head still, as it disarranged the pastry . . .

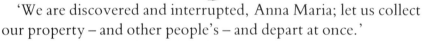

And a few pages later, when rescue is at hand for poor Tom:

'We are discovered and interrupted, Anna Maria; let us collect our property – and other people's – and depart at once.'

'I fear that we shall be obliged to leave this pudding.'

'But I am persuaded that the knots would have proved indigestible, whatever you may urge to the contrary.'

And so they depart, still arguing decorously like two clerics of Dr Johnson's day.

Beatrix Potter was probably an admirer of Johnson. She was certainly an avid reader of Jane Austen, and traces of both writers' styles appear in her work. But by the time of her penultimate notable book, *The Tale of Mr. Tod*, she is tackling themes that seem quite foreign to the age of Johnson, Austen, and her grandmother. *Tod* is not merely a dialect English word for 'fox', but the German for 'death', and this book, which announces itself blandly as dealing with 'disagreeable' people, is a study in murderous intentions.

Tommy Brock the badger intends to kill and eat the rabbit babies; Mr Tod the fox, finding Brock in his bed, is utterly delighted when he believes he has killed him; and at the conclusion Tod and Brock engage in a vicious struggle of which the conclusion (surely the death of both of them) is left for the reader to guess.

Though *Mr. Tod* is the blackest of Beatrix Potter's books, it is also the funniest. Nothing else in children's literature, and very little written for adults, comes near the hilariously macabre passage where Mr Tod, finding the badger in his bed, makes elaborate preparations for revenge on this infringement of private property, carefully suspending a bucket over the head of the bed, attaching it to a rope secured to a tree outside, and then filling it, jug by jug, with cold water – all the while Tommy Brock pretending to be fast asleep, watching with one eye, snoring industriously: 'The snores were almost apoplectic . . .' Trying to find some comparison, one thinks not of literary parallels but of early film comedies featuring such grotesques as Mack Sennett. The Potter story, of course, is heavily illustrated, but even without the pictures (which are, uncharacteristically, mostly in black and white) it would resemble the violent comedies of the silent monochrome cinema, the sort of film that was being made at the time *Mr. Tod* was published.

The final Potter story into which she put all her powers as writer and illustrator, *The Tale of Pigling Bland*, is equally cinematic. It takes place within a specific time-span – two and a half days – and the passing of time and the changing of the light are very precisely recorded:

> He glanced wistfully along the road towards the hills, and then set off walking obediently the other way, buttoning up his coat against the rain . . .

A little later on:

> After an hour's wandering he got out of the wood [note that 'got' again]; the moon shone through the clouds, and Pigling Bland saw a country that was new to him.

201

The road crossed a moor; below was a wide valley with a river twinkling in the moonlight, and beyond, in misty distance, lay the hills.

And towards the end of the story, when Pigling Bland and Pig-wig, the girl pig he has met at Thomas Piperson's sinister prison of a cottage, are escaping across the moors in hope of finding freedom in the next county – shades again of *Tess of the D'Urbervilles*, and an anticipation of all those thirties poems and novels about crossing the frontier – we see everything very clearly through the camera's eye:

He opened the house door quietly and shut it after them. There was no garden; the neighbourhood of Mr Piperson's was all scratched up by fowls. They slipped away hand in hand across an untidy field to the road.

The sun rose while they were crossing the moor, a dazzle of light over the tops of the hills. The sunshine crept down the slopes into the peaceful green valleys, where little white cottages nestled in gardens and orchards.

'That's Westmorland,' said Pig-wig.

We have come a long way from *The Tale of Peter Rabbit*.

The Tale of Pigling Bland – Beatrix Potter's *Persuasion* – expresses Beatrix's exhilaration at her own personal escape, in the year that it was published, from the family fold, and the freedom that her marriage granted her. (Like Anne Elliot in the Austen novel she had suffered an earlier tragic disappointment, when her fiancé Norman

Warne had died abruptly of leukaemia.) Though she lived for another thirty years, she published nothing further of importance. But though her work appeared only during the first thirteen years of this century she belongs to the modern age rather than the Victorian. There are moments when her work even bears resemblances to the modernists – her use of antiquated diction for motives of parody and social comedy has touches of Eliot and Joyce. The very least claim one may make for her is that she brought a precise diction and a vigorous use of English into books for very small children, which must have been an enormous influence for the good. There is some evidence that her deliberately flat, unemotional narrative voice, the characteristic cool Potter tone in which everything is expressed by understatement, helped to create the narrative style of Graham Greene's generation of writers – possibly including Evelyn Waugh. This paragraph, for example, could almost have been written by Beatrix Potter:

> Mr Sniggs, the Junior Dean, and Mr Postlethwaite, the Domestic Bursar, sat alone in Mr Sniggs' room overlooking the garden quad at Scone College. From the rooms of Sir Alastair Digby-Vane-Trumpington, two staircases away, came a confused roaring and breaking of glass. They alone of the senior members of Scone were at home that evening, for it was the night of the annual dinner of the Bollinger Club. The others were all scattered over Boar's Hill and North Oxford at gay, contentious little parties, or at other senior common-rooms, or at the meetings of learned societies, for the annual Bollinger dinner is a difficult time for those in authority.

'Confused . . . contentious . . . difficult': this sort of wry understatement seemed a new voice in English fiction in 1928, when Waugh's *Decline and Fall* appeared. Is it too fanciful to trace it back to those small books for young children which were appearing year by year during Waugh's childhood?

To most people Beatrix Potter is the creator of Peter Rabbit and his friends. Some others know of her exquisite watercolours and yet others of her detailed knowledge of fungi and of sheep breeding, her interest in china and furniture and her love of gardening. What is not so widely known or understood is her long association with the National Trust. Susan Denyer is the Historic Buildings Representative of the National Trust in the North West.

'THIS QUIXOTIC VENTURE': BEATRIX POTTER AND THE NATIONAL TRUST

SUSAN DENYER, 1992

WHEN BEATRIX Potter died in 1943, she was well-known in the Lake District as Mrs Heelis, farmer, Herdwick sheep-breeder and supporter of the hill-farming community. In her will she left to the National Trust her 4,000 acres of land, a huge estate including seventeen farms and eight cottages built up during the last twenty years of her life. Her legacy remains one of the largest and most significant ever made to the organization and it marked the end of a thirty-year association between Beatrix Potter and the National Trust. She had been spur, critic, helper and land agent and, above all, an ardent supporter of the Trust's work.

Beatrix Potter's close association with the National Trust was largely fostered by one man, Canon Hardwicke Rawnsley, Vicar of Wray and then of Crosthwaite, and one of the founders of the National Trust in 1895. They met in 1882 during the sixteen-year-old Beatrix Potter's first visit to the Lake District, and it was a friendship that lasted until his death thirty-eight years later. In the early years their mutual interest was writing for children. Rawnsley, author of the highly-successful *Moral Rhymes for the Young*, was influential in getting Frederick Warne to publish Beatrix Potter's first children's book, *The Tale of Peter Rabbit*, in 1902. Later, when she came to live in the Lake District, their interests

Beatrix Potter with Canon Rawnsley and his son Noel

again coincided in working to preserve the area against unsuitable developments.

When Beatrix Potter was in her twenties and thirties the Potter family travelled up from London every year to spend the summer in the Lake District, taking houses in and around Sawrey or Keswick. Beatrix Potter became particularly attached to Near Sawrey and to the 'quaint, old-fashioned residents'. In 1905 she invested all her profits from the five little books she had by then published, together with a minor legacy, in the purchase of Hill Top, a small working farm. She enlarged the house, building on a new wing for the farm tenant, and used the old farmhouse as her base for increasingly lengthy and regular visits to Near Sawrey from London.

Almost immediately she involved herself in the day-to-day workings of the farm, writing enthusiastically about it all in a letter to a friend:

The pigs are mostly sold – at what drapers call a 'sacrifice'; . . .
The whole district is planted out with my pigs; but we still take
an interest in them because if they grow well we shall 'get a name
for pigs'. Such is fame!

In 1909 Beatrix bought another farm in Sawrey, Castle Farm,
adding the land to Hill Top. In this and later purchases she sought
the advice of William Heelis, a partner in a local solicitor's office in
Hawkshead. Their friendship developed and in 1913 they were
married, setting up home in Castle Cottage, Near Sawrey. Beatrix
Potter had become Mrs William Heelis, Lake District farmer.

Her concern for her farmland and animals soon turned to
campaigning. In 1911 she drafted a letter in protest at what she saw
as 'grandmotherly legislation':

Under the amended law for the protection of animals it has
become illegal for a 'child' under 16 years of age to be present at
the slaughter and cutting up of carcases . . . do our rulers
seriously maintain that a farm-lad of 15½ years must not assist at
the cutting up? One of the interesting reminiscences of my early
years is the memory of helping to scrape the smiling countenance
of my own grandmother's deceased pig . . .

A year later her concerns became more local, her methods more
wide-ranging. She mounted a campaign to stop flying boats on
Windermere. She wrote to *Country Life* complaining of probable
'danger, turmoil and possibly pecuniary damage . . . at the hand of
fellow-man' to animals crossing on the Windermere ferry in that
'ramshackle, picturesque boat . . .' which might be caused by the
noise of the propeller of the hydroplane. She also organized a
petition, approaching publishers, farmers, doctors and nurses,
among others, for signatures. Her campaign was entirely successful;
it prompted a government inquiry and before the end of the year the
planes had left Windermere.

Beatrix Potter was becoming part of a long tradition in the Lake

District, for distinguished residents to use their names to campaign against what they saw as despoliation of their chosen home by later groups of 'off comers'. What drew Wordsworth, Southey, Ruskin and others to the Lake District was the same appreciation of the space, beauty and peace which later attracted larger numbers to settle in the area and millions to visit each year. The newcomers set in train changes that would threaten the character of the area which had enticed people there in the first place. The popularity which the Lake District began to enjoy brought with it, however, the seeds of its salvation: it had the ability to draw attention to itself and its problems.

By the end of the nineteenth century, the scale of tourism had drawn in its wake developers looking acquisitively for land for villas or guest houses. On the other hand, the almost magnetic attraction of the area created a ready audience for campaigns to stop development, amongst those who had made memorable visits and wanted to offer support. The signatories for Beatrix Potter's protest against flying boats included thirty-four doctors and nurses at a London hospital, of whom no fewer than thirty-one had visited the Lakes.

The catalyst for much of the action against unsuitable building in the early 1930s was the National Trust, which had been set up in 1895 to hold land for the benefit of the nation, in response to widespread concern over the loss of open spaces and public rights of way. Its early acquisitions in the Lake District were all bought with funds raised through subscriptions or specific appeals, and in 1907 the Trust was given the power through Act of Parliament to hold its land inalienably, a measure which gave a permanence to successful campaigns against development.

In the early days the National Trust's staff was minimal and, therefore, had to work through local committees or loose associations of people, drawn together to raise funds to allow action to be taken against a threat. After land had been purchased and vested in the National Trust, these same volunteers acted as local management committees.

In 1924, with the National Trust as well as herself in mind, Beatrix Potter again enlarged her farm holdings – but on a more dramatic scale, investing profits from her immensely popular little books, of which twenty-two had now been published. The spectacularly sited Troutbeck Park Farm at the head of the Troutbeck Valley covered 1,500 acres, rising from Troutbeck village in the south to the lowest slopes of the Kirkstone Pass in the north. The farm was under threat from developers who wanted to build houses on the bottom land.

Beatrix Potter sought to keep the farm together as a working unit, and almost immediately the purchase was complete she drafted a will leaving it to the National Trust. Two years later she wrote to Mr Samuel Hamer, Secretary of the National Trust in London, explaining how she would like the Trust to manage the farm after her death. The letter, setting out the 'desirable prospect' for the farm, gave observations on all aspects of the management of the land. She showed a keen eye for the details and diverse elements which together typify a Lake District farm: buildings, livestock, trees, fences, tenants, as well as the furniture in the farmhouse – 'Lakes housewives are accustomed to the care of old oak furniture'.

> *Tenants* . . . remember that a good intelligent solvent tenant is preferable to a rack rent . . . *Herdwick men are untidy farmers.* . . .
> *Sheepstock* . . . At present I am minded to fix the number of 'Landlord's stock sheep' at the number of 1100 sheep, viz 700 ewes, 180 twinters, 220 hoggs, all to be pure bred heafed Herdwicks.

By the mid 1920s, Castle Farm had become an object of pilgrimage for several American admirers, and Beatrix Potter had begun to correspond with others. In 1927, Cockshott Point, on the east side of Lake Windermere, came under threat of development. A group of local people started a subscription list to raise money for its purchase by the National Trust, and Beatrix Potter mobilized support from her New England friends, including Bertha Mahony of the Boston Bookshop. In May 1927, she sent fifty original drawings, copied from four of the illustrations from *The Tale of Peter Rabbit*, to Bertha Mahony:

> 'Beatrix Potter' has very much at heart an appeal to raise a fund to save a strip of foreshore woodland and meadow, near Windermere Ferry, from immenent [sic] risk of disfigurement by extensive building and town extension.
> So many nice kind Americans come through the Lake district on their tour, some of them ask after Peter Rabbit Do you think any of them would give a guinea . . . to help this fund, in return for an autographed drawing?

By November £100 had been raised, entered in the subscription list as from 'friends in Boston'. In the following spring Beatrix

Potter wrote with satisfaction 'the glebe land estate is quite secured now; . . . and it will be thrown open to the public next summer – to the great pleasure of strangers from the Lancashire mill towns who like to picnic beside the lake'.

Until the mid 1920s, the National Trust was acquiring discrete pockets of land and buildings bordering lakes or roads which had already been earmarked for development or redevelopment. Sometimes property was given, but at other times it was acquired through subscription. The severe economic depression of the 1920s heralded a distinct change of emphasis. Food prices slumped and land became available in quantity at affordable prices. The core of the Lake District, with its small farms, whitewashed houses and network of stone walls, reflecting an agricultural tradition comparatively unchanged since the Middle Ages, was increasingly vulnerable.

It was a threat Beatrix Potter had perceived when she bought Troutbeck Park Farm in 1924. Her purchase brought her into the realms of detailed land management and a direct involvement with the National Trust. In making her prescriptions for the way the Trust should manage Troutbeck Park Farm, she showed she understood that the gentle man-made landscapes of the Lake District, which are so pleasing to the eye, will only remain in essence unchanged if the farming system which created those landscapes in the first place is kept largely intact. For the next eighteen years Beatrix Potter became more and more immersed in the life and traditions of the Lake District as she, together with the National Trust, acquired farms under threat and managed them in the customary way.

The year 1929 was a watershed for both the National Trust and Beatrix Potter. The National Trust acquired its first farms: Stool End and Wall End Farms at the head of Great Langdale, and Cockley Beck and Dale Head Farms in the Duddon. In October that same year Beatrix Potter heard that the Monk Coniston Estate was being put up for sale. This large estate covered 2,500 acres of land to the north east of Coniston Water. Apart from seven farms there were also quarries, cottages, open fell land and the already famous beauty spot of Tarn Hows, a man-made lake set within plantations of exotic conifers created in the nineteenth century.

On 20 October 1929 Beatrix Potter wrote to Samuel Hamer to say she was interested in buying but 'I will say at once I cannot afford to present anything to the Trust, much as it would please me to do so – because this speculation means selling out what is the main stay of my income and replacing it by rents.'

The Trust immediately agreed to her proposal – that if she were successful in buying the whole, it would buy half of the estate from her once it had raised sufficient money. Moreover, the Trust asked her to negotiate on its behalf.

It was soon discovered that building development was not the only threat; the Forestry Commission was interested in buying the estate to clear off the timber and afforest the farm land. Beatrix Potter wrote again:

> There may have been disaster. Mr J. Marshall is afraid that his London solicitor Mr Owen has sold the whole to the Forestry Commissioners. . . . have you any means of approaching the Forestry Comms. to try and get the valleys. . . . it would be a terrible pity to do away with the little green farms and to cut down the remaining scrubly timber. . . . you may have to fight it out with the foresters 'pull d –, pull baker'. ['Pull devil, pull baker' is a reference to a tug of war depicted in many puppet shows.]

Finally, the negotiations were successful: Beatrix Potter was to keep Far End Farm, High Oxenfell Farm, High Park Farm and High and Low Yewdale Farms, Stang End Farm and High Water-head Farm. The National Trust was to get Tarn Hows, which Beatrix Potter found 'too theatrical for my own taste; like scene painting', High Tilberthwaite Farm, Holme Ground Farm, Low Hallgarth Farm, Low Tilberthwaite cottages and Yew Tree Farm.

To raise the money for its share the National Trust launched a public appeal – something of a new departure, the money for previous smaller purchases having been collected through subscriptions from people known to the Trust. Beatrix Potter was sceptical:

> I have been accustomed to solace myself with two misquotations from the Scriptures. 'Blessed are they that expect very little for they shall *not* be disappointed' and 'The Lord helps them that help (i.e. assist) themselves'
> . . . I still feel very averse to public begging; probably you will gradually get it in tens, twenties, hundreds amongst friends.

Nevertheless, the appeal was made public in a letter to *The Times* from John Bailey, Chairman of the National Trust, on 15 February 1930. Mr Bailey reported that £5,000 had already been raised from subscriptions, but that an extra £3,500 was still needed. Beatrix Potter congratulated John Bailey on his 'dignified appeal':

> Those of us who have felt the spirit of the fells reckon little of passing praise; but I do value the esteem of others who have understanding.
> It seems that we have done a big thing; without premeditation; suddenly; inevitably – what else could one do?
> It will be a happy consummation if the Trust is able to turn this quixotic venture into a splendid reality.

The money was raised and the National Trust asked Beatrix Potter if she would manage its half of the Monk Coniston Estate as well as her own. She wrote:

> . . . and I have a personal gratification – they have asked me to manage it for a time, 'til it is in better order; . . . – interesting work at other people's expense!

Letters continued to flow from Castle Cottage to Samuel Hamer as Beatrix Potter manoeuvred small pieces of the estate and her interest in land negotiations gained apace. In 1932 her profits from these small land sales enabled her to purchase Thwaite Farm, Coniston, adjoining the Monk Coniston Estate. Once again, she was buying to save the farm from building development although, for some reason, she did not like Thwaite Farm and announced that she would give it straight away to the National Trust, on condition that the gift was anonymous. Unfortunately, the gift was acknowledged as coming from Beatrix Potter in the National Trust's Annual General Meeting report for 1931. Immediately Beatrix Potter wrote to Samuel Hamer:

> . . . I am very much annoyed about it.
> You had better tell Prof. Trevelyan what . . . he has done. Willie and I had made up our minds to give a good deal more if my mother had died last time when she was so ill. *Now I won't*. It must take its chance.

Although Beatrix Potter was by now managing extensive areas of land for the National Trust she called herself an amateur land agent. Amateur she may have been, but she was certainly not remote. Over the next ten years she involved herself closely in the management of the estate: choosing tenants, repairing buildings, felling and replanting woodland and mending walls. She kept up a regular correspondence with Trust staff in London, explaining and debating her work, and she wrote in her usual forthright way: 'it's disagreeable to seem to be wiser than other people! But I cannot help saying what I think.' Not surprisingly her approach caused some consternation: Major Heyder, the National Trust's Forestry Adviser, was less than sympathetic to her wanting to deal with tree felling 'in her own way, on picturesque lines'. He wrote:

> Personally, I have always thought it somewhat odd that a lady, who has a perfectly competent husband, should insist on managing every detail of farm and woodland problems herself . . . but the National Trust do receive much of the

impetus to preserve picturesque areas of countryside from such odd personalities, and one must be tactful with them in return . . .

In choosing tenants, Beatrix Potter exercised a mixture of sensitivity and firmness. She re-let Yew Tree and Tilberthwaite Farms and numerous cottages. For farm tenants she appreciated the value of local men, although she had long thought Herdwick farmers were 'untidy'. Nevertheless, they knew how to gather sheep and cope with the inclement weather on the high fells. She cautioned against 'applications from any semi-genteel outsiders, it would be desirable to get a *very reliable* reference. Their morals are sometimes bad; or they are people who run (up) debts to tradesmen.'

Beatrix Potter was also a realistic conservationist: she understood that in hard economic times it was necessary to take the opportunities presented by the ever-increasing number of visitors to the Lake District. She encouraged tenants to offer accommodation, saying in a letter 'catering visitors seems to be the only chance of making farms pay'. And at Yew Tree Farm, Coniston, she set up a tea room at her own expense, buying in oak furniture and local paintings. She had an enlightened attitude, too, to the needs of those who came to visit from outside: 'The Lake District depends so much on tourists and visitors.' As an outsider herself she could understand the pleasure they derived: even in her late sixties she was writing spontaneously of her delight in it all: 'I was at Buttermere on Friday . . . The valley was as beautiful as a dream – wonderful – spring leaves and gorse in flower.'

She did not identify with the tourists, though, writing somewhat patronizingly, 'I think there is an undesirable class of daytripper comes to Coniston Village; . . . Rather a different class visits the Ghyll; fat women off chara's. They might fall through the bridge.' Nevertheless, she took a very businesslike attitude to their needs; she was not averse to creating car parks and picnic areas, and to putting up signs and litter bins. She gently reminded Samuel Hamer that such things had to be done appropriately. Hand-painted signs were sent up from London. On their arrival, she commented on the colours used: 'On thinking it over it occurred to me that cream and chocolate is likely to be conspicuous in this slate country.' She also expressed doubts about the carefully selected Roman lettering, pointing out that there were 'no living Romans left' to appreciate it.

Beatrix Potter had always foreseen that when the National Trust substantially increased its holdings in the Lake District it would want to appoint a full-time agent. She wrote forcibly to Samuel Hamer about the sort of person it should take on:

> . . . *an absentee landlord with a typical land agent*. I think that is the system that has made what socialism exists in the countryside. I thought you would have to have an agent sooner or later – but oh dear – oh dear! – Mr Hamer, I *did hope* he would be a gentleman. . . . Our Westmorland lads are rough; but you have no idea how sharp they are to reckon up whether a man is a gentleman or not. . . . The typical agent has the faults of the idle rich, with bumptiousness added.

In 1932 the National Trust appointed Bruce Thompson to manage its Lake District estates not looked after by Beatrix Potter. Six years later he took over the Monk Coniston Estate as well. Bruce Thompson worked for the National Trust for ten years and became well-liked, writing a history of the Trust's work in the area and gaining much respect in the community. But Beatrix Potter was not amongst those who thought highly of him:

> . . . A man cannot help having been born dull. Thompson is supercilious as well.
>
> He destroyed the finest group of oaks on Thwaite, dealing with a man he had been warned against.
>
> . . . He seems to have no sense at all. And not capable of learning. Indeed, excusably; because it is impossible to inculcate a pictorial sense of trees arranged in landscape, when imagination is a blank.

Beatrix Potter's complaints about Bruce Thompson say more about her than about the Trust's much-maligned agent. It was probably inevitable that any successor in running the Monk Coniston Estate would be resented by her, and letters of complaint flowed regularly to Bruce Thompson and Donald Matheson, Samuel Hamer's successor as Secretary in London. They were treated with consternation and circulated around the Estates Committee members. An uneasy truce prevailed. Beatrix Potter continued to offer advice and criticism to Bruce Thompson:

> We all have to learn by mistakes; I remember making plenty! I thought, since you mention it, that Holme Fell fence was a costly mistake. It is exactly the sort of wild open fell ground that ought and could be left open to the public.

And she commented to Donald Matheson:

> . . . As regards advice – a man must have judgement to sift the value of advice and of advisors, otherwise it is like the fable of the old man and his donky [*sic*].

Despite her annoyance with Bruce Thompson and other individuals connected with the National Trust, Beatrix Potter was able to look dispassionately at the organization and identify always with its aims. Never once did her loyalty and support waver. In addition to all her generosity and help, she continued to pay her subscription regularly. She took a long-term view of the problem:

> . . . The Trust is a noble thing, and – humanly speaking – immortal.
>
> There are some silly mortals connected with it; but they will pass.

Beatrix Potter's bequest to the National Trust included all her farmhouses, cottages and land. As well as Beatrix Potter's half of the Monk Coniston Estate, Troutbeck Park Farm and her farms in Near Sawrey, there were two more in Hawkshead, three in Little Langdale and one in Eskdale.

Beatrix Potter was the right person at the right time. She had the foresight to perceive the threat to the Lake District landscape, and to realize that only through ownership and control could its essential details be preserved. She also had the means to safeguard it. Her legacy to the National Trust and to the nation is only now beginning to be understood and appreciated.

ABOUT THE CONTRIBUTORS

BRIAN ALDERSON is a lecturer, translator and reviewer of children's literature in Britain and the USA. He is also the bibliographer of Edward Ardizzone and Maurice Sendak. His revision of F.J. Harvey Darton's *Children's Books in England* was published in 1983 and in 1986 he devised the Randolph Caldecott exhibition, *Sing a Song for Sixpence*, at the British Library.

DELMAR BANNER (1895–1983) was a Lake District artist who, as his widow says, 'painted the fells from the tops. He could paint *air*.' After his death the Victoria and Albert Museum bought three of his pictures and a large sketchbook for the nation.

HUMPHREY CARPENTER's books include *J.R.R. Tolkien: a biography* (1977), *The Oxford Companion to Children's Literature* (with Mari Prichard, 1984), *Secret Gardens* (1985) and a popular series of 'Mr Majeika' books for children. In 1983 he founded the band Vile Bodies, playing 1920s and 1930s dance music and jazz.

MURRAY CLELAND spent nearly four years in Britain during the Second World War, as a radar mechanic and then in Flying Control in Fighter Command. Returning to Canada he became a farmer in Meaford, Ontario, and the manager of a small plant producing 'that useful but humble article, the wheelbarrow'.

SUSAN DENYER, Historic Buildings Representative of the National Trust in the North West, was responsible for setting up the gallery of Beatrix Potter's watercolours in Hawkshead in 1988. Her books include *Traditional Buildings & Life in The Lake District* (1991) and a National Trust Souvenir Guide, *Beatrix Potter and Her Farms* (1992).

ANNIS DUFF (1904–1986) worked in the Toronto library system before becoming a children's bookseller. While bringing up her own children she taught in a nursery school, contributing articles to

The Horn Book which led to the publication of *Bequest of Wings* (1944) and *Longer Flight* (1955). Moving to New York in 1950 to become children's books editor at Viking, she retired in 1968.

JANE GARDAM's first book was for children, *A Long Way from Verona* (1971). She now writes novels and short stories for both adults and children and has won the Prix Baudelaire, the Whitbread Literary Award, the David Higham Award, the Winifred Holtby Award and the Katherine Mansfield Award. 'Some Wasps in the Marmalade' was a paper read to the Royal Society of Literature on 21 April 1977.

NICHOLAS GARLAND, born in London, was educated in New Zealand and at the Slade School of Fine Art, London. After some years in the theatre he has, since 1964, earned his living as a cartoonist and illustrator. With Barry Humphries he created and drew the Barry McKenzie strip in *Private Eye*, and he has contributed cartoons to *The New Statesman*, *The Independent*, *The Spectator* and *The Daily Telegraph*.

RUMER GODDEN, novelist and author of a number of memoirs, wrote *The Tale of the Tales* (1971), an account of the making of the Beatrix Potter ballet film. Her books for children include *The Dolls' House* (1947) and *The Diddakoi* (1972), both of which have been dramatized for television.

SELWYN GOODACRE is a General Medical Practitioner, and a book collector with over 1,500 copies of the *Alice* books. Editor of the Journal of the Lewis Carroll Society, he is the current Society Chairman. His 1991 Linder Memorial Lecture to the Beatrix Potter Society was entitled 'Beatrix Potter and Herbal Medicine'.

GRAHAM GREENE (1904–1991) published his first short story in 1921 and his first novel, *The Man Within*, in 1929. There followed a distinguished list of novels, short stories, plays and essays and four books for children, *The Little Train* (1947), *The Little Fire Engine* (1950), *The Little Horse Bus* (1952) and *The Little Steamroller* (1953).

ANNE STEVENSON HOBBS is Frederick Warne Curator of Children's Literature in the Special Collections section of the National Art Library, the Victoria and Albert Museum. Material in her care includes the Linder Bequest, the largest single collection of Beatrix Potter's art.

PAUL JENNINGS (1918–1989) was a regular contributor to *Punch* and *The Spectator* and on the staff of *The Observer* from 1949 to 1966. His 'Oddly Enough' columns were collected in a series of anthologies and he wrote three books for children, including *The Great Jelly of London* (1967).

MARGARET LANE, novelist, biographer and critic, was awarded the Prix Femina-Vie Heureuse for *Faith, Hope, No Charity* (1935). Her other books include *Edgar Wallace* (1938), *The Brontë Story* (1953) and *Life with Ionides* (1963). Her biography *The Tale of Beatrix Potter* was published in 1946 and *The Magic Years of Beatrix Potter* in 1978.

ANNE CARROLL MOORE (1871–1961) was for ten years children's librarian at Pratt Institute Free Library, Brooklyn, New York, and from 1906 to 1941 supervisor of work with children at New York Public Library. A pioneer of children's librarianship and a teacher of children's literature, she was also a children's book author and a frequent contributor to professional journals.

JANE MOORE (Jane Kingshill) is a professional stage designer and an amateur poet. She has for some time past been much involved with P.A.T.H., a theatre group integrating mentally and physically disabled actors with the non-disabled.

MARIANNE MOORE (1887–1972) was born in Missouri and her first book, *Poems* (1921), was followed by a number of other collections.

'I can see no reason for calling my work poetry except that there is no other category in which to put it,' she once wrote. *The Oxford Companion to English Literature* comments: 'Her poems are composed for the page with a strong sense of visual effect.'

CHARLES MORGAN (1894–1958) was the author of a number of novels including *The Fountain* (1932) and *The River Line* (1949). He was also a playwright, and from 1926 to 1939 he was the drama critic for *The Times*. His 'Menander's Mirror' pieces were published as *Reflections in a Mirror* (1944) and *Second Reflections in a Mirror* (1945).

ELAINE MOSS has been teacher, librarian, bookseller, publisher's reader, writer and critic. In 1977 she was the winner of the Eleanor Farjeon Award for distinguished services to children's books. 'The Audience for Children's Books' was her address to the Library of Congress International Year of the Child program in 1979 and was included in the collection *Part of the Pattern* (1986).

SUZANNE RAHN teaches children's literature at Pacific Lutheran University in Tacoma, Washington. She is the author of *Children's Literature: An Annotated Bibliography of the History of Criticism* (1980) and is Associate Editor of *The Lion and the Unicorn*.

MAURICE SENDAK, writer and illustrator of books for children, has won the Caldecott Medal, the Hans Christian Andersen Medal and numerous other awards. He is a designer of sets and costumes for opera and ballet and the founder, in the USA, of the national children's theatre *Night Kitchen*.

JANET ADAM SMITH was Assistant Editor of *The Listener* and Assistant Literary Editor of *The New Statesman & Nation*. Author of *Children's Illustrated Books* (1948) and editor of *The Faber Book of Children's Verse* (1953), she frequently writes on children's books for the *New York Review of Books*.

ALISON SMITHSON studied architecture at the University of Durham. Her best known work, in partnership with Peter Smithson, is the Economist Building in London and their best known project the British Embassy in Brasilia. She is a frequent contributor to professional architectural publications.

NICHOLAS TUCKER is a lecturer in child psychology at the University of Sussex, and has been writing and broadcasting about children's literature for the last twenty-five years. Evacuated to Sawrey in 1940, he believes he saw Beatrix Potter 'bent over in her garden, looking very much like Mr McGregor'.

ROSEMARY WELLS was born in New York City and 'raised by an English/Australian father and a pan-European mother'. She wrote and illustrated her first children's book in the early 1960s and *Noisy Nora* in 1973. Her award-winning 'Max' board books were published in 1979. She also writes mystery novels for teenagers.

DOROTHY NEAL WHITE was awarded a Carnegie scholarship to study in Pittsburgh, USA, after four years in the Canterbury Public Library in New Zealand. From 1937–44 she was children's librarian in Dunedin Public Library and then librarian at Dunedin Teachers' Training College. Her critical study of children's literature, *About Books for Children*, was published in 1946 and *Books Before Five* in 1954.

ACKNOWLEDGEMENTS

The author and publishers are grateful to the following for permission to reproduce material in this book: Frederick Warne for *Meeting Beatrix Potter*, Anne Carroll Moore; David Higham Associates for *Beatrix Potter: A Critical Estimate*, Graham Greene (© Verdant S A 1966, 1968, 1969) (*Collected Essays*, the Bodley Head, 1969); Janet Adam Smith and Frederick Warne for *The World of Beatrix Potter*; E. M. Cleland for *With Kind Regards*; Josephine Banner for *Memories of Beatrix Potter*, Delmar Banner; Margaret Lane and David Higham Associates for *The Ghost of Beatrix Potter* (*Purely for Pleasure*, Hamish Hamilton, 1966); Jane Moore for *Crime in Beatrix Potter*; Viking Penguin, a division of Penguin Books USA Inc., for the extract from *Bequest of Wings*, Annis Duff (copyright 1944, renewed © 1972 by Annis Duff); Dorothy Neal White and the New Zealand Council for Educational Research for extracts from *Books Before Five*; Elaine Moss for the extract from *The Audience for Children's Books*; Jane Gardam for the extract from *Some Wasps in the Marmalade*; Rumer Godden for *An Imaginary Correspondence*; Maurice Sendak, Farrar, Straus & Giroux Inc. and Reinhardt Books Ltd for *The Aliveness of Peter Rabbit* (published in *Caldecott & Co.* under the title *Beatrix Potter/2*, copyright © 1988 by Maurice Sendak); Faber and Faber Ltd and Viking Penguin, a division of Penguin Books USA Inc., for *Tell Me, Tell Me*, Marianne Moore (copyright 1960, renewed © 1988 by Marianne Craig Moore, *The Complete Poems of Marianne Moore*); Alison Smithson for *Beatrix Potter's Places*; Suzanne Rahn and the Yale University Press for *Tailpiece: The Tale of Two Bad Mice* (*Children's Literature*, vol. 12, edited by Francelia Butler and Compton Rees, copyright © 1984 by the Children's Literature Foundation Inc.); *The Observer* for *Oddly Enough: On Beatrix Potter Translated*, Paul Jennings; Nicholas Tucker and the Beatrix Potter Society for *Some Further Adventures: Peter Rabbit and the Child Psychologist*; Christopher Preston, M. Lewis Jones, Jane Thurston-Hoskins and Judge Peter Fox for letters to *The Times*; Times Newspapers Ltd 1990 for *Crimes of Peter*

Rabbit; Anne S. Hobbs and Frederick Warne for *Beatrix Potter's Other Art*; Rosemary Wells for *Sitting in Her Chair* (copyright © 1991, all rights reserved, used with permission); Nicholas Garland for *'Controlled Wool-gathering': The Political Cartoonist and Beatrix Potter*; Brian Alderson for *'All the Little Side Shows': Beatrix Potter Among the Tradesmen*; Selwyn Goodacre for *'Peter Rabbit and His Ma': Collecting Beatrix Potter Piracies*; Humphrey Carpenter for *Excessively Impertinent Bunnies: The Subversive Element in Beatrix Potter*; Susan Denyer and the National Trust for *'This Quixotic Venture': Beatrix Potter and the National Trust*.

ILLUSTRATION
ACKNOWLEDGEMENTS

Illustrations and photographs are reproduced by kind permission of the following: the Trustees of the Linder Collection, Book Trust, pages 13, 137; private collections, pages 16 (above), 21, 41, 63, 110, 205, 208; the National Trust, pages 16 (below), 45, 66; the Armitt Trust, page 17; the Frederick Warne Archive, pages 99, 155, 157, 163, 217; the National Art Library, Victoria and Albert Museum, pages 138, 140; the Rare Book Department, Free Library of Philadelphia, page 143; Nicholas Garland, page 153.

All other illustrations are taken from Beatrix Potter's books, published by Frederick Warne.